Sunset

Roofing & Siding

BY THE EDITORS OF SUNSET BOOKS AND SUNSET MAGAZINE

*Cedar shake roof and painted lap siding are fitting materials
for this modern version of a Stick-style house. Decorative
latticework at the gable end accentuates the entry.
Architect: John B. Scholz.*

Sunset Publishing Corporation ■ Menlo Park, California

Salmon-toned cedar siding harmonizes with variegated asphalt roofing. Posts and custom gable end give this duplex a distinctive appearance.

Book Editor
Lynne Gilberg

Research & Text
Don Vandervort

Coordinating Editor
Sarah T. Hudson

Design
Joe di Chiarro

Illustrations
Bill Oetinger
Mark Pechenik

Photographers: ABTco, Inc.: 33 bottom, 34 bottom left, 35; *Alcan Building Products:* 42 top; *Alcoa Building Products:* 19 middle, 38 right, 39 top, 40 right, 41, 42 bottom, 43 top and bottom; *American Hardboard Association:* 32 top, 34 top; *American Wood Council:* 13 top, 14 top; *American Plywood Association:* 15 bottom, 33 top, 48; *Brick Institute of America:* 44 bottom; *Cal-Shake, Inc.:* 18 bottom; *Carter Holt Harvey Roofing USA, Inc.:* 19 bottom; *Cedar Shake & Shingle Bureau:* 13 right; *CertainTeed Corp.:* 9 top, 38 left; *Glenn Christiansen:* 10 top, 43 middle; *Classic Products, Inc.:* 23 bottom; *Dryvit Systems:* 44 top; *Michael Garland:* 45 middle; *Green River:* 8, 22; *Phil Harvey:* 14 bottom; *George Lambros Photography:* 23 top; *Louisiana-Pacific Corp.:* 32 bottom; *Ludowici-Celadon, Inc.:* 17 bottom; *Renee Lynn:* 19 top; *Manville/Schuller:* 10 bottom; *Jack McDowell:* 17 top; *Met-Tile, Inc.:* 21 top right; *Owens-Corning Fiberglas Corp.:* 11; *Norman A. Plate:* 45 top; *Rocky Mountain Log Homes:* 31 bottom, 45 bottom; *Shakertown:* 36 bottom; *Chad Slattery:* 16 top; *Southern Forest Products Association:* 12 top, 24 top; *Tegola USA:* 21 top left; *Roger Turk/Northlight Photography:* 12 bottom, 16 bottom, 44 middle; *Brian Vanden Brink:* 1, 2, 4, 9 bottom, 21 bottom, 24 bottom, 25 right, 28, 29, 30 top and bottom left, 31 top, 36 top, 37, 39 bottom, 40 left; *Don Vandervort:* 15 top, 18 top, 25 left, 34 bottom right; *Western Red Cedar Lumber Association:* 30 bottom right.

Editor, Sunset Books: Elizabeth L. Hogan

First printing January 1994

Your Best Investment

Have you taken a close look at your home's roof and exterior walls recently? If they're showing signs of wear, maybe it's time to consider replacing or repairing their surfaces. If you wait for the next major storm to convince you, your repairs may multiply.

And consider how good your house could look. When worn shingles are covered by courses of new, neatly laid shakes, or when weary walls are refreshed with a layer of new siding, a house is transformed. Old becomes new, drab becomes striking. Tired looks give way to a fresh, bright appearance.

This book is a guide to replacing and maintaining your home's roofing and siding. A photo gallery provides the inspiration and information you'll need to choose the most appropriate materials. Sections of how-to information on roofing and siding guide you, step by step, through the techniques of planning and installing common roofing and siding materials. You'll also find helpful advice on how to repair and maintain roofing and siding for years of lasting protection.

We thank Beronio Lumber for supplying props for the cover photo and Donald E. Johnson, Building Official of Menlo Park, for his careful checking of this edition. Our special thanks go to Marcia Morrill Williamson for carefully editing the manuscript and to JoAnn Masaoka Van Atta for photo styling.

Cover: Today's choices of roofing and siding materials include (clockwise, from top left) fish-scale shingles, asphalt shingles, glazed ceramic tiles, redwood clapboard, fir plywood, and Spanish clay tile. Cover design by Williams & Ziller Design. Photo styling by Sudi Scull. Photography by Colin McRae.

CONTENTS

THE ESSENCE OF SHELTER

Nothing feels quite as cozy as a snug house in a storm. Though rain runs down the windows, hail hammers the roof, and wind wails against the walls, you can relax inside in the comfort of a warm, weathertight home. On the other hand, nothing leaves you feeling quite as vulnerable as the "drip, drip" of a leaky roof.

Without a doubt, the most important duty of a house is to shelter its inhabitants. And no parts of the house are more important to this function than its major weather barriers, its roof and its siding.

Roofing and siding are also important in defining a house's architectural character: wood shingles give a natural look; clay tile suggests a Southwestern or Mediterranean style; clapboard conveys tradition.

Today's market offers a wide variety of roofing and siding products, each with its advantages and drawbacks. Many are the result of recent technology, developed to address homeowners' needs in new ways. For example, if you like the appearance of board siding but would prefer a lower-cost, lower-maintenance alternative, you'll be pleased to learn about the new easy-care metal and vinyl sidings

Standing-seam metal roofing blends beautifully with horizontal cedar siding on this handsome residence. Architect: Dave Allen.

that offer the look of wood without the expense. Or you might find yourself drawn to one of the new high-tech roofing materials designed to resemble wood shakes but to cost less and to resist fire.

This book has several purposes. First, if you want to replace roofing or siding, it can help you evaluate the sometimes confusing array of available materials and make an appropriate selection; the chapters "Selecting A New Roof" and "Selecting New Siding" offer extensive information on materials, as well as color photographs that show how the products look in place. Second, if you need to install or repair roofing or siding, it helps you take a realistic look at the skills and tools required, then guides you through the procedures step by step.

Beginning on page 48, you'll find advice on how to attack your project—starting with inspecting roofing and siding to determine its condition and identify any problems. This chapter will help you decide whether or not it's feasible to do your own work and help you work successfully with any professionals you decide to hire. It also discusses code requirements and related concerns.

Information on roofing preparation begins on page 56: this chapter explains how to estimate and order materials; how to tear off existing roofing and/or ready the roof deck to receive new roofing; how to flash a roof; how to install skylights; how to

allow for ventilation; and more. Instruction in do-it-yourself roofing begins on page 74; repair and maintenance techniques start on page 88.

The discussion of siding preparation takes up on page 94, with siding installation instruction beginning on page 100 and siding repair and maintenance information on page 114.

ROOFING & SIDING: A BRIEF PRIMER

Whether you're just shopping or planning to install roofing or siding yourself, in order to understand relevant literature and talk intelligently with dealers and contractors, you'll need a working knowledge of construction methods and terms. This guide will get you started. For more about roofing terms and wall-related terms, refer to the chapters on preparation and installation.

Anatomy of an exterior wall

A house wall's frame is usually constructed with 2-by-4 or 2-by-6 studs (see page 6). Insulation is placed between the studs, which are then covered with a sheathing of wood-based panels or insulation board. Depending on the type of siding to be applied, building paper or house wrap (see pages 97–98) may be applied over the sheathing to provide additional weatherproofing.

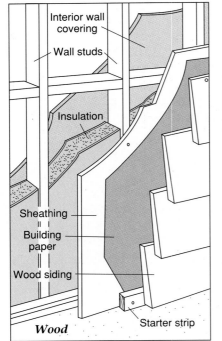

Interior wall covering
Wall studs
Insulation
Sheathing
Building paper
Wood siding
Starter strip

Wood

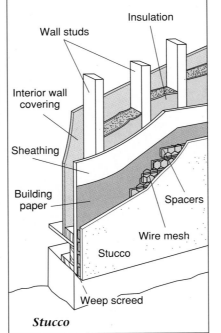

Wall studs
Insulation
Interior wall covering
Sheathing
Building paper
Spacers
Wire mesh
Stucco
Weep screed

Stucco

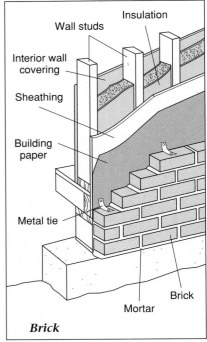

Insulation
Wall studs
Interior wall covering
Sheathing
Building paper
Metal tie
Brick
Mortar

Brick

For wood siding, the boards are then nailed on, lapped from the bottom up to allow for water runoff.

For standard stucco siding, wire mesh is nailed directly to sheathing covered with building paper or to spacers (as shown above). Stucco is applied over the wire mesh in three layers. In a contemporary variation on this time-honored method, many contractors now install stucco-like systems that use special backerboards with polymer-based coatings.

For masonry walls, a veneer of brick or stone is attached to the underlayment (building paper) with short metal strips called ties. Then the bricks or stones are mortared in place. Their weight is supported by part of the foundation.

Anatomy of a roof

Roofs are built in a variety of shapes; some of the more common forms are shown on the facing page. Typically, a framework of rafters supports a roof

deck (sometimes called a subroof) consisting of sheathing and underlayment. The roof deck provides a base for nailing on the roofing surface material.

The roof deck. Though the type of deck used may vary, depending on the surface material to be applied, most decks consist of both sheathing and underlayment.

The sheathing, the nailing base for the surface material, is usually composed of solid plywood but may consist of spaced boards if certain materials, such as wood shingles, are to be used.

Sandwiched between the sheathing and the surface material goes the underlayment—a heavy, asphalt-saturated black paper that is thick enough to resist water penetration from outside, yet porous enough to allow moisture from inside the attic to escape.

The roof surface. What's on top of the roof must be able to withstand wind, rain, snow, hail, and sun. You

can choose among a wide variety of surface materials; see pages 8–27.

On pitched roofs, materials are applied in horizontal layers, called "courses," which overlap one another from the eaves to the ridge. The portion of the material exposed to the weather is called the "exposure," and the edge that is down-roof is called the "butt." Asphalt shingles, the most common roofing surface,

MEASURING 3-IN-12 PITCH

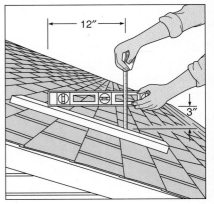

12"

3"

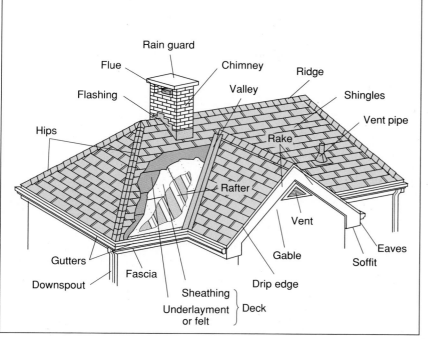

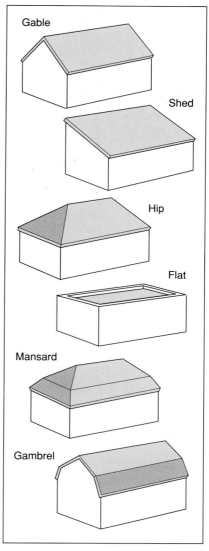

Gable

Shed

Hip

Flat

Mansard

Gambrel

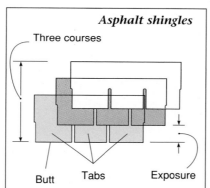

Asphalt shingles

Three courses

Butt   Tabs   Exposure

are divided into sections called "tabs."

Roof pitch is a term used to express the ratio of a roof's vertical rise in inches to each foot of run—the horizontal distance. A "3-in-12 pitch" describes a roof that rises 3 inches vertically for every foot (12 inches) of horizontal distance.

The surface of a roof is often broken by angles and protrusions, all of which require weatherproofing—usually provided by flashing. Made from malleable metal or plastic, flashing forms the drip edge along the eaves and rakes of a roof, the collars around ventilation and pipes, the valleys between two roof planes, and the "steps" along a chimney or dormer. It's also used to protect other breaks in the roof's plane, such as those around skylights.

At the roof's edges, gutters made of metal, wood, or vinyl catch runoff and channel it to downspouts, which direct the water away from the house and safely into the soil.

QUICK REFERENCE GUIDE

SELECTING
A NEW ROOF

I f you've just begun to shop for new roofing, expect to find a staggering range of choices. The offerings stretch well beyond the old stand-bys, asphalt shingles and wood shakes, to a vast array of mason-ry, metal, and composite hybrids. You'll discover fibrous cement versions of shakes and slates, clay and concrete tiles (as well as metal tiles coated with granulat-ed stone), copper-surfaced asphalt shingles, and zinc-finished ribbed steel panels—just to name a few. You'll even find shake-like panels made from recycled computer housings.

How do you choose? Appear-ance certainly is important, but you'll also need to weigh some other factors, such as the cost, durability, and fire rating of the material and the degree of slope of your roof. The following pages will introduce you to the various products; to compare their char-acteristics, see pages 26–27.

Split cedar shakes add a crowning touch to an elegant country home. Copper roofing accents bay windows. Design: John F. Buchan Homes. Product design: Green River.

ASPHALT-BASED SHINGLES

A sphalt-based shingles (also called composition or "comp" shingles) cover about 80 percent of all American homes. They owe their popularity to a number of qualities: they're economical, widely available, easy to apply, relatively lightweight, fire resistant, and easy to maintain. And they last longer than most people own their houses—from 12 to 40 years. Premium-grade asphalt shingles look fine on most houses, though some homeowners prefer a heftier, more richly textured look.

To manufacture asphalt shingles, mats made from either wood

Premium asphalt-fiberglass shingles imitate slate quite convincingly. At 430 pounds per square, this product is among the heaviest and thickest on the market, offering heavy shadow lines and long-term performance. Product design: CertainTeed Corp.

Like undulating eyelids, mounded roof forms roll over curved window and the arched entry of this boathouse. One of asphalt's pluses is its flexibility—here it flows easily over rounded forms. Architect: David Sellers, Sellers & Co.

▪ ASPHALT-BASED SHINGLES

pulp and paper fibers or fiberglass are covered, top and bottom, with protective layers of asphalt, then coated on top with mineral granules of various colors. What you see on the finished roof is the mineral coating.

Organic-base asphalt shingles (commonly called asphalt or comp—for composition—shingles) have felt mats made of wood and paper fibers. Fiberglass-base asphalt shingles (called fiberglass shingles) employ a fiberglass base for the mat. They have better fire ratings than organic-base shingles (UL Class A compared to Class C—see page 26) and longer warranties.

All composition shingles are sold by the square (enough to cover 100 square feet) and come in many textures, colors, and weights. Standard shingles are divided into three sections, or tabs, and measure 12 by 36 inches (some manufacturers make a metric-system equivalent which, in inches, measures 13¼ by 39⅜). Two-tab shingles have two 18-inch tabs, creating a more horizontal line that tends to make a roof look lower and longer. Most asphalt shingles are made with a self-sealing mastic strip that fastens one tab to another after the shingles are installed, preventing wind lift.

Rolling around a turret, asphalt shingles tie addition to the original portion of this house. Architect: Robert Anderson, Schacks Architects.

Variations in the gray and black tones of this premium asphalt-fiberglass roofing create a heavily textured look. This product weighs in at 360 pounds per square and carries a 40-year limited warranty. Product design: Manville/Schuller.

Colors run from crisp white to dramatic black and include a range of rich earth tones as well as subtle hues of red and green. You can even buy types that have been laminated with copper foil (see page 21). Some conventional composition shingles are embedded with fungus- and algae-resisting zinc granules to serve in warm, humid climates.

Standard shingles weigh 220 to 235 pounds per square. Premium-weight types, which have a three-dimensional appearance more like that of wood shingles, weigh up to 430 pounds per square. Shapes range from the traditional rectangular butts that give a roof a smooth, clean appearance, to the random-edge butts that provide a more rustic look.

Specialty shingles—such as 9- by 12-inch ridge shingles—are also available. In some areas, you may see wind-resistant interlocking ("T-lock") shingles or 12- by 18-inch "Dutch-lap" units.

Asphalt roofing is also manufactured in the form of roll roofing, 36 inches wide and 36 feet long, with a mineral-grain surface. It's used on outbuildings and economy housing with pitches as low as 1 in 12, or in a matching color to cover the valleys of an asphalt-shingle roof.

With blended earth tones of rust, gray, and white, reinforced fiberglass shingles play with light, color, and texture. Like other asphalt-fiberglass products, this roofing has a Class A fire rating. Product design: Owens-Corning Fiberglas Corp.

Random tabs and bands of dark granules combined with bright colors change the look of this architectural asphalt-fiberglass roofing at different times of day. Like a number of other quality asphalt materials, these shingles come in 13¼-inch by 39⅜-inch units that cover more quickly and economically than standard-size products. Product design: Owens-Corning Fiberglas Corp.

WOOD SHINGLES & SHAKES

When it comes to appearance, few roofing materials can match the natural beauty of wood shingles and shakes. Most wood shingles and shakes are cut from Western red cedar, though you can also buy kinds made of Eastern cedar or preservative-treated pine—and if you look hard enough, you might even be able to find shingles of redwood, cypress, and oak.

Shingles, with their smooth, finished appearance, are sawn from chunks (called bolts) of wood. They come in lengths of 16, 18, and 24 inches.

Southern pine taper-sawn roof shakes, pressure-treated with CCA preservative, are a viable alternative to cedar shakes. Properly treated, they'll last at least 30 years, and are not prone to cupping or splitting.

Natural cedar shakes, silvered with age, provide a fitting cap for a traditional residence. Though shakes give long-term service untreated, they hold up even longer when coated with a fungicide in damp climates or treated with an oil-based preservative in dry climates.

Contemporary home takes advantage of the natural look of shingles— one of the few roofing materials that seem appropriate with nearly every style of architecture, Colonial to cutting edge. Design: American Wood Council.

Shakes are thicker, and though some are sawn from bolts, most are split by machine or by hand into 18- and 24-inch lengths. You can buy two different weights, medium and heavy, and several styles, such as hand-split, hand-split and resawn (smooth on one side), and taper-split (tapered).

Hand-split shakes generally last longer than machine-split shakes because the wood fibers haven't been sawn through and are thus less likely to rot. Even so, either type will last from 15 to 25 years—or longer—if carefully maintained. In humid climates, new shingles should be treated with a fungicide after about one year. You can also apply a clear wood preservative and fungicide, using a garden sprayer, every two to five years (don't use a product that seals the wood).

Though shingles and shakes are available in several grades (suitable for siding as well as roofing), you should be sure to specify Number 1 ("Blue Label") grade for use on a roof. The best ones are straight-grained heartwood (from the most durable, sap-free part of the tree).

Where fire is a particular threat, shingles and shakes that have been pressure-treated with a fire retardant are advisable, if not mandatory. Such shingles have a Class B fire rating when applied over a solid deck of ½-inch plywood or a Class C rating when applied over open or solid wood sheathing. The only way to get a Class A fire rating is to apply retardant-treated shingles over a deck of special gypsum and sheathing. Untreated shingles or those treated with only a spray-on coating will burn like kindling in a fire.

Three kinds of cedar roofing include the hand-split and resawn shake (left); the shake resawn on both sides (center); and the thinner shingle, also sawn on both sides (right).

■ WOOD SHINGLES & SHAKES

For decorative treatments, you can also buy fancy-butt shingles, 5 inches wide and 16 or 18 inches long, in several different shapes—from half-cove to fish-scale patterns. Though these are most often used on exterior walls, they're occasionally woven into a roof design to add a touch of interest.

Most shingles and shakes are nailed on one by one, making application somewhat labor intensive (though the materials are easy to handle). You can also buy shingles pre-nailed in 4- or 8-foot panels for faster installation.

On roofs, it's best to apply shingles over open sheathing, allowing plenty of air circulation underneath them to prevent rot. Where necessary, they may be applied over solid sheathing if they're raised off the deck about an inch by furring strips for ventilation.

Hand-split shakes may be applied directly over an existing asphalt-shingle roof. Shake liner underlayment goes under each course to create a watertight barrier.

Wave coursing produces a highly distinctive cottage-style roof. Installation calls for very short exposures—an average of about 3 inches—and irregular butt lines. Special framing and steam-bent shingles are required. This roofing is best reserved for steeply pitched roofs on authentic European-style cottage homes; on anything else, it can look contrived. Roofing design: Forrest Construction & Roofing.

MASONRY ROOFING

Masonry materials, though relatively expensive, are prized for their handsomeness and long-term durability. In this category, the two classics are natural slate and ceramic tile; fibrous cement and concrete tiles or shakes are popular new variations.

SLATE

Natural slate is a stone quarried in New York, Pennsylvania, Vermont, Virginia, and in other countries. Grade and color depend on the stone's origin. Installation of slate requires a skilled craftsman, and because the material is heavy, the roof may need to be beefed up to provide extra support (professional advice may be needed to determine where this is necessary). Expect to pay several hundred dollars per square for a new slate roof.

TILE

Ceramic tile comes in the rounded Spanish-style terra-cotta familiar in the Southwest, California, and Florida and in a wide range of other styles and colors. Glazed "Traditional French," "Oriental," and other patterns are available in dark greens, blues, burgundy, and other rich tones. Because tile is an expensive material ($200 or more per square),

Concrete tiles have lugs that hook onto battens fastened to solid sheathing. Tile edges interlock. Vent flashings are worked into courses as the roof is installed. Product design: Monier, Inc.

Faux slate, actually fibrous cement tile, has consistent widths but irregular butts and variegated color, like the real thing.

quite heavy, and difficult to install, it's best left to a professional roofer. Tile is also prone to breakage.

CONCRETE & FIBROUS CEMENT

Manufacturers now offer a wide selection of tile and slate look-alikes, created from a mixture of asbestos-free fibrous cement and concrete. These are just as durable as tile and slate, and considerably more affordable. They are highly resistant to rot, insects, wind, hail, and fire.

Concrete tiles are made in the classic Spanish barrel and S shapes and in flat, shake-like patterns. Fibrous cement shakes tend to be flatter, lighter in weight (some have a perlite base), and more convincing imitations of slate and shakes. They are easier to install, and they're more forgiving of foot traffic.

Masonry tiles come in several sizes, including 9½ by 16, 12 by 17, 12 by 22, and 16 by 20 inches. Most

Spanish clay tile is by far the most appropriate roof for classic Spanish- or Mediterranean-style architecture. It's beautiful and—if you don't walk on it—can last many decades.

Slate roof, capped with a copper ridge, is the height of elegance and durability—some slate roofs have lasted for several hundred years. Accordingly, it's the most expensive roofing material of all. Architect: Ed Weinstein. Remodeler: Shultz-Miller.

are from ½ to 1 inch thick, and many have interlocking edges. Some have lugs on their bottoms that hook over battens nailed to solid decking. Manufacturers also supply accessory ridge, hip, and rake tiles.

GENERAL CONSIDERATIONS

If you're considering roofing with any masonry product, weight is the most critical factor. Most masonry materials weigh 900 to 1,000 pounds per square—three or four times as much as asphalt shingles—and your roof must be sturdy enough to handle the load. You can buy "light-

As green as the hills, glazed ceramic tile roof sheds everything Mother Nature can dish out. Bold colors are available in this material. Product design: Ludowici-Celadon, Inc.

These Spanish-style clay tiles have been in place since the house was built in the 1920s. They've been painted black for an elegant look.

■ MASONRY ROOFING

weight" concrete tiles or fibrous cement shakes that run about 550 pounds per square.

Check with your building department to see if you'll need an engineering report; your house may require additional structural bracing. Also be sure to read the manufacturer's literature; some concrete and fibrous cement tiles are susceptible to cracking in areas with frequent freeze-thaw cycles.

You may also want to estimate shipping charges if you live a considerable distance from the manufacturer. Tile costs more than most other roofing materials and is expensive to ship because of its weight.

Hips and ridge of concrete tile roof are finished with special angled tiles. Such roofs are among the heaviest, at about 900 pounds per square; in many cases, structural reinforcement is required. Product design: Monier, Inc.

Imitation slate tiles of fibrous cement with a perlite base weigh about 560 pounds per square. They may be score-cut, sawn, or fastened like wood shakes. On pitches of 4 in 12 or greater, they may be applied over open sheathing. Though not recommended for locations with dramatic freeze/thaw cycles, the brand shown, when properly installed, has a 50-year limited warranty. Product design: Cal-Shake, Inc.

METAL ROOFING

T hough metal roofing was once reserved mostly for use on barns and commercial buildings, new developments in materials, finishes, and manufacturing techniques have made metal panels, imitation wood shakes, tile and slate look-alikes—even Victorian metal tile re-creations—popular for residential roofing.

TYPES OF METAL

Steel and aluminum are the two metals most commonly used for roofing, but others include stainless steel, copper, and zinc alloys. *Steel* is a favorite because it's sturdy and relatively inexpensive. To keep it from rusting or corroding, it often has a multilayered finish: a zinc-galvanized base coating, a sealer, an epoxy primer, and a baked-on acrylic top coat (sometimes embedded with stone granules to yield realistic imitations of wood and tile). Corrugated galvanized steel is an inexpensive alternative for noncorrosive climates (but don't use it near the ocean); if you don't like its silvery surface, you can paint over it.

   Stainless steel is impervious to rust and corrosion, but it's very expensive and far too shiny for roofing. It is, however, used for some luxury-home roofs when coated with terne (an alloy that's 4 parts lead to 1 part tin), which gives the steel a soft, matte gray color. If you choose this type of roof, be aware that rain runoff, particularly when the roof is new, will carry some lead. Because of the toxic effects of ingested lead, don't install a terne-coated roof if you rely on well water or grow produce near the house.

Snow slides right off this steeply pitched standing-seam roof. Multilayered finishes on sheet-metal panels offer a broad palette of color with long-term durability. Architect: John Malick.

Aluminum shake roofing looks right at home on this contemporary house. At a mere 50 pounds per square, aluminum roofing is a featherweight material that won't rot, rust, split, warp, burn, or break. Product design: Alcoa Building Products.

Steel shake-style roofing has a multilayered finish with a surface of stone chips. Steel roofing doesn't burn, rot, or break. Installed only by authorized dealers, it weighs 150 pounds per square and carries a limited 50-year warranty. Product design: Carter Holt Harvey Roofing USA, Inc.

More common terne-coated roofing has a base of prime copper-bearing steel, coated with terne on both sides and painted with a terne paint (all joints are solder-sealed, and paint adheres exceptionally well to the terne coating). This is a time-tested technique that has been used on American roofs since the early eighteenth century.

Aluminum is a favorite for houses. It won't rust, and it's very lightweight; but to improve its appearance, it must be painted or coated with the same types of finishes as those used on steel.

Copper is a beautiful, ageless roofing material that may last for centuries. Left unfinished, it weathers naturally to a verdigris patina. Unfortunately, copper is very expensive. Some homeowners reserve it for accents such as small roofs over porches or bay windows.

A few specialized roofing materials are made from *alloys* formulated for strength, graceful weathering, and durability. As a group, alloys are quite expensive.

BENEFITS & DRAWBACKS OF METAL

In comparison with other materials, metal roofing excels in several areas. For one, it lasts a long time. A properly installed metal roof should shed snow, repel rain, and survive high winds for as long as the house stands. Though warranties vary, most companies back their materials for from 20 to 50 years.

Metal roofing resists fire, insects, mildew, and rot. Though it heats up quickly on a sunny day, many types employ foam insulation fillers or are installed with dead air space to increase their insulation value (and, fortunately, metal cools quickly at night). Temperature fluctuations cause metal roofs to expand and contract substantially; for this reason, most are attached with fasteners that allow for movement.

Metal roofing products are relatively lightweight. Some can be applied over one or two existing roofs without removing existing shingles or adding strengthening support members. Fire ratings, however, depend on the nature of the deck beneath the metal. Most metal tile roofs achieve a Class A rating if applied on a new roof deck. If they're put directly over an old roof, they receive a Class C rating. If they're installed with heavy roofing felt between old and new roofs, they get a Class B rating.

Most products are meant to be installed by qualified metal-roofing contractors. A few types can be handled by homeowners (see page 84).

What about disadvantages? Products that imitate tiles or shakes are not always convincing in appearance. In a rainstorm, a few types may be noisy—and metal roofing could conduct electricity from a lightening strike and so must be grounded. Some kinds of aluminum roofing will dent in a hailstorm. And some metal surfaces scratch or dent if walked on.

Often the biggest disadvantage is initial cost—metal is costly to buy and also to install. If you plan to live in the house for a long time, however, it should repay the investment with long, virtually maintenance-free performance.

PRODUCT TYPES

Metal roofing materials come as both shingle-type systems and larger sheet-metal systems. For shingle systems, the metal is usually em-

Standing-seam sheet metal caps a short arcade, providing a simple and appropriate transition between original house, with cedar shakes, and new, metal-roofed garage addition. Sheet-metal roofing works particularly well on simple roofs. Architect: John B. Scholz.

Laminated copper on asphalt-fiberglass shingles yields a copper roof at a fraction of the cost of all copper. This material, with either rounded or square butts, ages to a verdigris patina. Product design: Tegola, USA.

Painted steel, with a stucco-like finish, is installed in up to 20-foot lengths that reach from eaves to ridge. Stepped design encourages ventilation beneath roof. Product design: Met-Tile, Inc.

bossed with a tile- or shake-like texture and formed into panels that interlock. Most panels are about 4 feet long; you can also buy shingles made for individual application, which are easier for homeowners to install. Panels can often be applied over an existing roof, but individual shingles need a firm, flat base and usually require tear-off.

Sheet or "ribbed" roofing systems, once used only in commercial or industrial situations, are now an accepted material for homes. Roofing manufacturers form "flat stock"—in most cases, flat sheets of 26-gauge steel—into large, durably finished roofing panels and parts.

Some sheet-metal roofing is fabricated on the spot by sheet-metal contractors, but these types don't offer as wide a selection of possible finishes as manufactured products and are subject to wide variations in quality. You're also less likely to be able to get the protection of a long-term warranty.

Because of the large size of the panels, sheet-metal roofing works best on large, unbroken expanses where minimal cutting is required. Panels may be ordered to cover the full distance from peak to eaves without a joint.

The two main sheet-metal systems derive their names from the methods used to join the panels. "Standing-seam" roofing has a self-sealing, raised seam that is crimped after it's in place, and "batten" roofing has a seam that's covered by a cap. With either system, matching parts are available for ridges, hips, edges, and connections.

Sheet-metal roofing is typically priced by the square foot. Figures quoted by qualified installers usually —but not always—include all necessary materials and labor.

To prevent condensation from collecting beneath sheet-metal panels, they are usually installed over spaced sheathing, battens, or a special type of ventilation matting.

Copper canopy covers bay windows simply and elegantly. Though copper is an expensive roofing material, using small amounts as detailing can add affordable distinction to a home. Design: John F. Buchan Homes. Product design: Green River.

Terne-coated standing-seam roof contributes a natural matte gray patina to a very contemporary home. Also popular for historic restorations, terne dates back to the early eighteenth century. Architects: Youngman & Co., Inc. Product design: Follansbee Steel.

Durable aluminum-shingle panels interlock to provide a weather-tight roof. Because of their light weight, they may be installed over some existing roofs, eliminating tear-off. Finishes come in several colors. Product design: Classic Products, Inc.

FLAT & LOW-SLOPE ROOFS

Flat and low-slope roofs—those with a pitch of 2 in 12 or less—need materials that completely seal out ponding water. Over the past decades, the most common of these has been built-up roofing—also known as "tar-and-gravel" or "hot-mopped" roofing. More recent innovations are single-ply roofing and, for some situations, polyurethane foam.

BUILT-UP ROOFING

The typical built-up roof consists of several layers of fiberglass-base asphalt sheeting, each coated with mopped-on hot bitumen. After the uppermost layer is coated, it is surfaced with crushed rock or gravel to minimize the damaging effects of the sun (some types utilize a colored cap sheet). Built-up roofing is priced by the number of layers applied; the more layers, the longer the roof will last, and the more it will cost. Most built-up residential roofs consist of three layers and achieve a Class A fire rating. Regardless of the number of layers, installation is critical: a careless job will be short-lived.

SINGLE-PLY ROOFING

Single-ply roofs utilize a range of synthetic membranes that vary both in their particular properties and in the installation methods they require. Which to choose depends on the nature of your roof, how long you want your new roof to last, the material's availability in your area, and, of course, cost. It's best to call several roofers and review the options.

Elegant porch of classic Colonial home uses wood shakes on the pitched portion and a single-ply, modified bitumen roof on low-slope areas out of view from below.

Under wooden roof deck is a watertight, single-ply membrane. Drains collect water runoff and deliver it to downspouts. Decking is fastened to a loose grid of preservative-treated 2 by 4s so no fasteners penetrate the roof.

Single-ply roofs fall into three broad categories: modified bitumen, elastomers, and thermoplastics.

Modified bitumen. A modified bitumen or "torch-down" roof is very durable and quite handsome. It would be a good choice for an almost flat roof that may receive some foot traffic. For this type of roof, which must be applied over new solid sheathing, reinforced rubber-like sheets are rolled out, overlapped, and heated with a torch so that they virtually melt together to form a single membrane.

Elastomers. Several types are used for roofing. Unless you use the acronyms, the list is a true challenge in spelling and pronunciation: EPDM (ethylene-propylene-dienemonomer), CSPE (chlorosulfonated polyethylene), PIB (polyisobutylene), and the less formidable-sounding neoprene. All of these materials are laid in sheets. Each has its advantages: for example, CSPE comes in more colors than neoprene; EPDM stays flexible even when cold; and PIB is rugged (but can't be applied over an old asphalt roof). Again, discuss the choices with several roofers.

Thermoplastics. PVC (polyvinyl-chloride) is the most common roofing thermoplastic. It is tough and fire resistant, but less resistant to weathering than some of the elastomers, particularly EPDM.

POLYURETHANE FOAM ROOFING

For a polyurethane foam roof, trained applicators spray liquid plastic onto a roof's surface. As the spray dries, it expands to form a dense, seamless, waterproof skin with a high insulation value. Polyurethane can be applied to nearly any type of surface, including curved and irregular forms, though smooth, flat surfaces yield the best appearance.

When buying such a roof, you pay by the inch—thicker polyurethane provides more insulation but will cost more.

Polyurethane foam roofing can actually be applied on nearly any surface, but it's generally reserved for flat or low-slope roofs where it isn't highly visible; this is because it usually looks white and lumpy, as though the roof were covered with snow. Because the foam disintegrates with exposure to sunlight, it must be coated with a special type of paint and recoated every few years.

Torch melts the backing of modified bitumen roof before it's laid in place. Once installed, the joints are sealed with more heat.

In clear view from second-story windows and decks, single-ply EPDM roof has an attractive covering of semi-smooth graded stone. The stone provides ballast to keep roofing flat and protects it from ultraviolet degradation. (Note: Even "flat" roofs need a minimum pitch of ¼ inch in 1 foot for drainage.) Design: Anthony DiGregorio.

Buyer's Guide to Roofing Materials

Which roofing material is right for you? This chart can help you decide. Be sure to consider the following:

Cost. Prices can range from about $40 per square for basic asphalt shingles to $700 or more for slate. Material and labor costs vary by region, but as a rule, the simpler the roof lines, the lower the cost.

Freight can be a factor. Heavy materials or those that come from far away may be prohibitive. Also, some materials are easier to load, cut, and apply.

When figuring the cost of a roof, consider its life. You may save money in the long run by starting with better materials that won't require replacement in 10–15 years.

Weight. Concrete tile can weigh as much as 1,000 pounds per square; aluminum may weigh as little as 50 pounds per square. Lightweight materials are easier to handle and often may be installed directly on two previous roofs. Heavy roofing material usually calls for complete replacement and may also require structural reinforcement.

Material	Weight (pounds per square)	Durability (years)	Fire rating
Asphalt fiberglass shingles	220–430	15–40	A
Asphalt-organic shingles	240–300	12–20	C
Wood shingles and shakes	140–350	20–40	A—treated with special gypsum roof deck system; B—treated with solid sheathing; C—pressure-treated with fire retardant; none, untreated
Tile (concrete and clay)	900–1,000	50+	A
Tile (fibrous cement)	550	30–50	A or B
Slate	900–1,000	50+	A
Metal shingles (aluminum)	50	50+	A, B, or C
Metal shingles (steel)	100–200	50+	A, B, or C
Metal panels	45–75	20–50	A, B, or C
Asphalt roll roofing	90–180	5–15	A, B, or C
Built-up and single-ply	150–650	10–40	A, B, or C
Sprayed polyurethane foam	20 per inch of thickness	25+ (with proper maintenance)	A

Durability. Be sure you know how long the material is warranted. Check the type of coverage offered if a material fails (the actual life of your roof will depend on design, quality of materials and installation, local conditions, and so forth). Know the shortcomings of any material you consider—for example, concrete tile and some metal roofing can be damaged if you walk on them.

Fire ratings. Roofing materials are rated by Underwriter's Laboratories (UL) for their resistance to fire from outside the house. Class A rating means the material is effective against severe exposure; Class B will not catch fire under moderate exposure; Class C will resist only slight exposure. A material such as untreated wood shingles does not qualify for a rating. The type of deck beneath the roofing material often affects its rating.

Recommended slope. Materials are divided into those designed to shed water on a nearly flat roof and those meant for pitched roofs. (All materials will protect a steeply pitched roof but only a few will seal out water on a nearly flat surface.) Materials are rated by minimum slope.

Color. A dark roof will attract heat; a light-toned roof will reflect it. Where summer heat is more of a problem than winter cold, light-colored roofing is a good idea. Where winter warmth is the main concern, a darker roof is better.

Recommended minimum slope	Merits	Drawbacks
4 in 12 and up	Wide range of colors, weights, textures; economical; easy to apply; durable; low maintenance	Brittle when applied in temperatures below 50°F
4 in 12 and up	Wide range of colors, weights, textures; economical; easy to apply; durable; low maintenance	Less durable and fire resistant but almost equal in cost to fiberglass-base shingles
4 in 12 and up; down to 3 in 12 with reduced exposures	Natural appearance; easy to apply; durable; low maintenance	Flammable unless treated with fire retardant; moderately expensive; time-consuming to apply
4 in 12 and up; down to 3 in 12 with additional underlayment	Extremely durable; fireproof; available in a variety of shapes and tones	Costly to ship and install; requires sufficient framing to support weight; can crack
4 in 12 and up; down to 3 in 12 with additional underlayment	Extremely durable; fireproof; available in a variety of shapes and tones	Moderately expensive to install
4 in 12 and up	Extremely durable; fireproof; attractive	Very expensive; costly to ship and install; requires sufficient framing to support weight; may become brittle
4 in 12 and up	Lightweight; fire resistant	Can be scratched or dented
3 in 12 and up	Relatively lightweight; fire resistant	Can be scratched or dented
1 in 12 and up	Lightweight; durable; low maintenance	Expensive to apply to complex roofs
1 in 12 and up	Economical; easy to apply	Drab appearance
0 in 12 and up	Most waterproof of all	Requires professional installation
0 in 12 and up	Watertight surface; good insulation value; lightweight	Must be professionally applied; quality depends on applicator; can deteriorate

SELECTING NEW SIDING

The most significant exterior building material in terms of setting a tone for your home's appearance is siding. When siding is in disrepair, a house looks shoddy; when siding is crisp and well maintained, a house looks sharp. If your house's face has been sagging, flaking, or just generally falling apart, you can give it a real lift with new siding.

Of course, siding must do more than just look attractive. It must protect your house from wind, rain, and cold. And you'd like it to do this job with a minimum of maintenance.

When selecting a siding material, pick one that is durable, easy to maintain, complementary to your house's architectural style, and within your budget. For a comparative look at the benefits and drawbacks of various materials, see pages 46–47.

Natural cedar bevel siding blends with standard and decorative cedar shingles and standing-seam roofing to imbue a traditional farmhouse with classic style. Architect: Michael Wisniewski.

WOOD-BOARD SIDING

Painted cedar bevel siding emphasizes a contemporary home's horizontal lines. Bold corner, gable, and eaves trims create smart, clean, weathertight transitions. Architect: Stephen G. Smith.

Board siding seems as American as apple pie. It's ready availability, natural appearance, and adaptability to a wide range of styles have made this siding so popular that it has served as the standard for many years. Wood siding is manufactured in a variety of species, grades, patterns, and sizes. Synthetic products developed during the past two or three decades are designed to imitate the appearance of this beloved material.

Unfortunately, scarce supplies have driven up the cost of wood-board siding, particularly for premium species and grades. Another problem with wood siding is maintenance: stained or painted finishes must be renewed every few years. And the fact that wood is a natural product means it doesn't always behave as you'd like it to: it can split, warp, or burn.

Vertical tongue-and-groove siding accentuates the upright lines of a two-story contemporary home. White trim provides a bold accent for Western red cedar siding that has been treated with a natural finish. Architect: John B. Scholz.

SPECIES

Cedar and redwood, sold throughout most of the U.S., are preferred for their natural resistance to decay; other sidings are made of cypress and white pine. You may also find a number of local species, including spruce, Douglas fir, hemlock, Ponderosa pine, and yellow poplar. If you're trying to stretch your budget, check out local species that are in good supply. Be sure to install them properly and give them a protective finish, such as paint (some local woods will take paint better than cedar or redwood).

Be aware that decay resistance in woods, such as redwood and cedar,

Classic Colonial, trimmed in white, proudly displays natural cedar bevel siding. Application is the traditional New England treatment: 2½-inch exposures at the base grow to 4 inches at the top, giving the wall more protection where it's needed. Architect: Warren Hall.

depends on which part of the tree the wood is cut from. Heartwood, the darker wood found near the tree's center, is far tougher than the lighter-toned sapwood found near the bark.

The quality of the siding also depends on the age of the tree from which it's milled. Old-growth redwood and cedar yield tight-grained, knot-free wood that's about as rare—and costly—as platinum. Unfortunately, the wood from younger trees, though much commoner and cheaper, splits and warps more easily and won't take a finish as well.

GRADES

There are big variations in price and appearance from one grade to another. Terms used in grading often depend upon the species. Top grades may be called "Clear," "B and Better," "Select," "Clear Heart," "A Grade," or "Number 1." Lesser grades are "Select Knotty," "Number 1 Common," "Number 2 Common," and so forth. Talk with your lumber dealer about the species you're interested in; better yet, take a look at a stack of the material if you can.

Be sure the material you choose is free from pitch pockets; avoid any wood that is warped or has wane (bark defects) along the edges. If you plan to stain the siding, be aware that a grade with some knots will cost about half the price of a top grade—but that you'll have to seal all the knots if you want to paint the siding.

Moisture content also affects wood's performance. You can buy siding either kiln-dried or "green." Kiln-dried wood has a stabilized moisture content of 12 to 20 percent and won't shrink much. But green wood, with a higher moisture content, will shrink and may warp, espe-

New England barn-red siding adds charm and distinction to contemporary adaptation of a mill. The 8-inch Eastern white pine shiplap siding is a local material. Galvanized steel standing-seam roof, weathered to a gray sheen, recalls metal barn roofs. Architects: Theodore + Theodore.

By cladding the structural steel beams and posts as well as the house itself with cedar bevel siding, the building's strong, angular lines are emphasized. Architect: Stephen G. Smith.

Western red cedar narrow-bevel siding with contrasting trim lend charm and sophistication to this home. Paint permits use of less-than-perfect grades. This cedar is an excellent base for paint.

cially if boards are wide. All wood siding should be stored at the site for a few days before installation so it can adjust to local humidity.

PATTERNS & SIZES

Wood siding is sawed from a log so that it presents either "flat" or "vertical" face grain. Vertical grain changes minimally with seasonal changes in moisture content, and it will hold a painted finish longer; but you'll pay dearly for it.

Boards come rough-sawn or smooth. The wood may be surfaced on any of its sides, though the most common form is "S-4-S," surfaced on four sides.

Though some siding patterns are milled in uniform thicknesses like regular boards, most are milled with special overlapping or interlocking edges and in beveled or tapered profiles. The types that lock together, such as tongue and groove, don't allow for expansion or contraction and so are more prone to problems. Though most patterns are meant to be installed horizontally, some are milled for vertical installation (see page 102). For aesthetic reasons, vertical siding is usually reserved for low-slung contemporary homes and bungalows, and horizontal siding is used on most other houses.

Widths run 4, 5, 6, 8, 10, and 12 inches; boards are given nominal dimensions before drying and milling, so each size actually measures about ½ inch smaller. Widths of 8 inches or narrower shrink less and don't have the same tendency to cup as wider sizes.

Innovative diagonal board siding is made of Vermont native spruce clapboards, presoaked in a preservative stain and applied with only 2½-inch exposures. Architects: David Sellers/Bill Rienecke, Sellers & Co.

Log cabin siding looks like full logs but is actually 5½-inch-thick half-logs screwed to a wood-framed, plywood-sheathed wall. Mortar chinking is packed between logs for weathertightness. Design: Rocky Mountain Log Homes.

WOOD-BASE SIDING

Many of today's siding materials are by-products of the lumber industry. They are made up of thin wood veneers, wood chips and shavings, and/or sawdust bonded together under pressure with special resins and glues. These products include plywood, hardboard, and oriented-strand board (OSB) sidings, which are manufactured both as large sheets and as lap panels. The sheets measure 4 feet wide by 8, 9, or 10 feet long. Lap panels, which imitate the look of wood-board lap siding, are 6 to 12 inches wide by 16 feet long. In many cases, sheet sidings can give a house adequate shear strength without wall bracing.

PLYWOOD SIDING

Plywood siding consists of an odd number of wood veneers glued together in cross-laminated layers. You can buy panels or lap siding with a brushed, rough-sawn, or texture-embossed surface. Panels may have a variety of grooves, from V-grooves to deep channels. Common thicknesses are $^{11}\!/_{32}$, $^3\!/_8$, $^{15}\!/_{32}$, $^1\!/_2$, $^{19}\!/_{32}$, and $^5\!/_8$ inch. Face veneers include Douglas fir, redwood, cedar, and Southern pine.

Though most plywood siding is sold unfinished, redwood plywood is usually mill-treated with a water repellent. You can stain or paint plywood.

Plywood siding is graded according to the number of patches required to repair the surface in manufacturing. The best has no patches; the worst has no end of patches. The patches may be wood, synthetic resin, or both. If you plan to stain the plywood or give it a transparent finish, patches can look blotchy and

Hardboard panel siding, paired with a stucco-system wall covering, provides contrast and visual interest on contemporary facade. Hardboard was selected for its economy, paintability, and ease of installation. Architect: Carter Lee Redish. Product design: Masonite.

Woodgrain-embossed oriented-strand board (OSB) lap siding looks like cedar but won't warp or split and is much less expensive. Available in 6- to 12-inch widths, the material comes factory-primed, but you must finish it with paint or stain. Product design: Louisiana-Pacific Corp.

Plywood siding panels install quickly, provide structural support, and can be either painted or stained like wood. On this contemporary home, the walls are sided with APA medium-density overlay panels with grooves spaced on 4-inch centers.

unsightly. But they're smooth and flat enough to disappear under a coat of paint, and by buying a low grade of plywood and painting it, you can save substantially on material costs.

HARDBOARD & OSB

Hardboard and OSB sidings are popular alternatives to board siding because they are much less expensive, yet convincingly imitate wood when painted. You can choose from either smooth or embossed textures; you can even buy panels that look like cedar shingles or stucco. They don't have knotholes, voids between layers, or other such defects.

Prefinished stucco panel siding has realistically textured surface, including trowel marks. Because this material comes in 4-by-8 and 4-by-9 panels, false posts and beams or other techniques must be used to conceal panel edges. Product design: ABTco, Inc.

OSB panels are stronger than hardboard because of their construction: they're made of several layers of strand-like fibers that are saturated with a special binder and compressed at right angles to one another under extreme heat and pressure.

The nemesis of both of these materials is moisture, which can seep into panel edges and cause damage. Most are edge-sealed and factory-primed to help them repel moisture. All hardboard and OSB must be painted, either at the factory or on site, and all cut edges must be sealed. Factory finishes are so tough that many manufacturers warrant their products for 20 years. Some factory-finished types are sold with matching nails, though certain types are made to be blind-nailed, which looks better and helps keep water out.

Panel sizes are 4 by 7, 8, 9, 10, 12, or 16 feet, and $\frac{7}{16}$ inch thick. Lap sidings come in 6-, 8-, 9½-, and 12-inch widths and 16-foot lengths.

Textured beaded lap siding, 8 inches wide by 16 feet long, is made of hardboard. It is heat- and pressure-sealed with resin and linseed oil; then panels are primed. Product design: ABTco, Inc.

Painted hardboard lap siding, embossed with realistic wood grain, does an excellent job of imitating its pricier cousin, cedar. Because hardboard is a manufactured material, it has neither the natural flaws—nor the natural character—of real wood.

Plywood siding hugs the contours of a rounded wall. For easy bending, ⅜-inch-thick panels were applied over ⅜-inch plywood sheathing. Semitransparent, green-toned stain protects the plywood. Architect: Tony Unruh.

New home echoes traditional "plantation" style with the help of 8-inch-wide beaded lap hardboard siding. This siding is smooth, free of imperfections, and easy to finish. Product design: ABTco, Inc.

Hardboard bevel lap siding comes in 12-inch-wide panels with a multi-lap profile. Precise edges lock out moisture and are self-aligning. Panels come primed but not painted. Product design: ABTco, Inc.

WOOD-SHINGLE SIDING

Wood shingles and shakes are very popular as siding for many house styles, including Cape Cod, Shingle, Victorian, and Craftsman. The shingles and shakes are the same as those used for roofing, but lower grades can be applied as siding. They are discussed in depth on pages 12–14.

In addition to stock made for roofs, you can get a variety of specialty shingles and shakes for walls. Or you can buy "sidewall shakes"—actually shingles that have been given deep, machine-grooved faces, parallel edges, and straight ends. They're sold unfinished or pre-primed.

You can also buy cedar shingles factory-attached to plywood panels. These 8-foot-long sections install in a hurry and yield a professional-looking result.

Cedar shingles and shakes are flammable, like all wood products, so look for ones that have been factory-treated with a flame retardant.

Cedar shingles fit into a wooded setting beautifully. This contemporary home provides an excellent illustration of how shingles can roll around a curve. These were treated with a natural sealer to add protection and prevent uneven weathering. Architect: Stephen G. Smith.

Staggered-butt application of shingles gives homes a rural appearance. These shingles come as 8-foot-long, 2-course panels, pre-attached to plywood. Product design: Shakertown.

When properly cared for, painted cedar shingles and spruce clapboard siding can withstand the test of time. This classic 1890 farmhouse still proudly wears its original materials, recently restored. Vermont slate roof is also original. Restoration: Northern Architects.

Decorative diamond-butt shingles accent the walls of a new home with traditional style. A painted finish like this one mutes the natural look of wood shingles. Architect: John B. Scholz.

VINYL SIDING

Vinyl siding is one of the most popular alternatives to board siding. This is because it is relatively inexpensive (about a fourth of the cost of premium wood siding), easy to maintain, and reasonably convincing at imitating the look of wood. Like lap siding, standard vinyl siding is applied horizontally; but it goes up faster because each panel represents two or more 4-, 6-, or 8-inch-wide lapped boards. Panels are 12½ feet long.

Extruded from polyvinylchloride (PVC) and embossed with imitation wood grain, this siding is resilient and resists denting. It doesn't show scratches, since the color is mixed into the material (darker tones, however, are likely to fade in time). Vinyl won't rust, rot, or be eaten by termites, though it can become brittle in extreme cold. It resists fire but will burn when ignited. Though vinyl never actually needs to be painted, you can paint over it if you want a color change.

Fish-scale shingles—of vinyl—highlight the gable ends of this home's facade. Primary siding comes in double 4-inch-lap sections, each 12½ feet long. Product design: Alcoa Building Products.

Varying both color and pattern, contemporary home capitalizes on vinyl siding's broad palette. Because color is formulated into the product, vinyl won't peel or wear off. Product design: CertainTeed Corp.

Makers of vinyl siding have developed many accessories that form complete siding systems. Siding panels fit snugly into molded inside and outside corner pieces. Special trim hides the edges of panels below windows and soffits and fit panels around windows and doors. Among some of the other accessories are starter strips, drip caps, and soffit panels (see page 40).

In addition, some styles of vinyl are manufactured with insulation backings or equipped to accept drop-in insulation panels.

Brown vinyl lap siding does an excellent job of mimicking wood on the stately traditional home at right. Product design: Alcoa Building Products. Vinyl comes in many colors and patterns, with smooth or wood-grain finishes. Horizontal vinyl lap siding on the contemporary home below is crisp, weathertight, and easy to maintain. Architects: Sargent, Webster, Crenshaw & Folley.

Decorative Outdoor Millwork

Whether your house's style is traditional or contemporary, a sure way to add character and interest to its facade is to install decorative architectural millwork.

Though decorative filigree, gingerbread, moldings, and columns were historically made of wood by millwork shops and finish carpenters, a wide variety of millwork—both simple and ornate—is now manufactured from polymers, fiberglass, and aluminum. You can get nearly any type of pattern or profile—and some manufacturers will create custom patterns to your specifications.

Unlike traditional moldings, which are often built up from several pieces, many of these products are one-piece units, designed for easy installation. Some are components for new vinyl or aluminum siding systems; others are installed independent of siding. Because they utilize materials that are less expensive than wood and require less labor, synthetic moldings cost about 30 percent less than wood. And of course they stand up to weather much better.

Polyurethane Millwork

High-density polyurethane foam is molded to create a wide variety of architectural details. It's easy to cut and fasten with standard woodworking tools, yet it isn't subject to shrinkage, warping, decay, or other problems associated with wood millwork. Most polyurethane millwork is sold factory-finished, treated with a UV-inhibiting primer

and white acrylic finish that may be painted or stained with a non-penetrating stain.

Among stock products, you can buy decorative window headers and panels for under windows, mantels, pediments, door surrounds, scrollwork brackets, gable-end trim, corner trim, shutters, cornice moldings, and dentil blocks.

Siding Accessories

Manufacturers of vinyl and some aluminum siding fabricate architectural detailing to match their siding systems. Decorative corner posts, door and window surrounds, dentil molding, shutters, and similar decorative millwork

components are among their offerings, as well as shingle and siding patterns. Check manufacturers' catalogs (see "Information Sources," page 126, for what's available).

Wooden Millwork

If you intend to finish your trim with a clear sealer or transparent stain or if you want to renovate your home in a manner consistent with its original construction, you may prefer wooden millwork. You can buy and combine standard pieces or, if you're willing to pay the price, you can have pieces custom made. Components available as stock include turned porch posts, corner brackets, railings,

Sunburst pediment and flanking panel pilasters define the entrance for a cedar-sided Colonial home. Classic millwork is made from clear pine and cedar. Architect: Warren Hall.

Open louvered shutters and fish-scale shingle panels at gable ends add interesting detail and flair to vinyl-sided home. Product design: Alcoa Building Products.

and wooden ornaments. Woods most commonly used for moldings are pine and fir; either should be treated with preservative and painted. Though cedar and redwood are softer than fir, those species resist decay naturally.

Columns

Some columns are structural, whereas others are purely cosmetic. Nonstructural columns, made in various classical shapes, are formed from polymers (some are designed to receive structural posts). They're sold in increments of 4-foot lengths; you can choose from an assortment of decorative bases and capitals. Structural columns are made from wood, aluminum, or fiberglass composites.

Wood ones are made in cylindrical, tapered, and square shapes and come with a separate decora-

tive wooden base and cap. Surfaces may be fluted or styled in other ways. The wood is usually pretreated with preservative; it must be painted. Common sizes run from 6 to 20 inches in diameter and 8 to 20 feet in length.

Structural extruded-aluminum columns are primed with a special bonding primer and may have a factory finish. You can paint or lacquer them to match your house trim. Their construction is hollow, generally assembled from interlocking sections or staves. They come 8 to 30 inches in diameter, in lengths up to 30 feet.

You can also buy load-bearing hollow columns that are formed from a mixture of fiberglass, ground marble, and polymer resin (be sure to find out how much weight they can bear). These look like stone but are lightweight. Sizes range from 8 to 12 inches in diam-

eter and 8 to 18 feet in length. You buy capitals and bases separately.

Parts & Pieces

Are you familiar with the terms used to describe architectural components? Here is a brief primer.

■ *Brackets* are filigree or ornate cross braces or blocks between a vertical support, such as a post, and a horizontal member, such as a mantel.

■ *Capitals* are the top parts of columns or pilasters.

■ *Corbels* are short blocks that project out from a wall, often to hold a horizontal member.

■ *Cornices* are the constructions at the tops of walls, under the eaves.

■ *Dentil blocks* or dentil molding are toothed (indented) blocks or molding attached to a wall.

■ *Headers*, like mantels, are horizontal projections over the tops of windows or doorways.

■ *Keystones* are wedge-shaped blocks in the center of a header or mantle.

■ *Mantels*, like headers, are horizontal projections over the tops of doorways or over fireplace openings.

■ *Pediments* are rounded, peaked, or other decorative panels above doorways.

■ *Pilasters* are decorative vertical columns on each side of a doorway, usually flat against a wall or frame.

Vinyl door surround system, paired with tall wooden columns in a rounded portico, makes a stunning entry for a traditional home. Product design: Alcoa Building Products.

Pilasters, pediments, posts, and other molded millwork transform otherwise ho-hum entryway into an elegant and inviting focal point. Design: Alcoa Building Products.

METAL SIDING

Aluminum and steel sidings have come a long way since the infamous materials hawked by "tin men" in the 1940s and '50s. New metal sidings have successfully married functionality with good looks. In imitating wood, however, some metal sidings are still flawed by overly shiny finishes and poorly machined textures.

Horizontal patterns of aluminum and steel sidings are made to resemble bevel or lap siding. Vertical patterns have a board-on-board look. The number of durable baked-on and coated finishes available is nearly unlimited. Though these finishes may be warranted for 20 years or more, some may fade and scratch. When steel siding scratches, it will rust unless touched up.

Aluminum is easier than steel for the do-it-yourselfer to install because it's much lighter in weight and easier to cut and bend. It's also softer and more prone to dent than steel. Both aluminum and steel resist fire, rot, and insects. Because both conduct electricity, they must be properly grounded.

Trimmed with decorative millwork (see pages 40–41), aluminum can be an attractive low-maintenance siding. Product design: Alcan Building Products.

Steel siding offers durable protection, resisting hail and extreme heat. It won't rot, split, crack, or deteriorate like wood. You can buy fish-scale panels and other coordinated accessories. Product design: Alcoa Building Products.

Aluminum siding systems include all necessary corner, soffit, and window trim. Embossed with an artificial wood grain, aluminum siding is durable, won't rust, and requires little maintenance. Product design: Alcoa Building Products.

Galvanized corrugated sheet metal and board-and-batten siding make this house, a crisp geometric interpretation of a gabled barn shape, seem both contemporary and traditional. This type of galvanized sheet metal is very affordable and goes on quickly but needs careful attention to flashing and edge detail. Design: Jon Fernandez.

Up close, steel siding has an embossed wood grain that resembles wood siding, but the metal's surface tends to give away its true identity. It has a super-tough PVC finish. Product design: Alcoa Building Products.

STUCCO SYSTEMS & MASONRY VENEERS

Because of their long-lasting toughness and substantial look, several masonry materials are popular for siding houses. These include stucco and stucco-like systems and brick and stone veneers.

STUCCO SYSTEM

Conventional stucco is a mixture of cement, sand, lime, and water. It's churned into a thick paste and troweled onto a sheathing paper containing metal lath or mesh that has been attached to wall studs.

It's applied in three coats: a scratch coat as a base, a brown coat, and a finish coat, which may be textured or smooth and is usually colored or tinted. Because each coat must be allowed to cure properly before the next one goes on, stucco siding can be fairly expensive and time-consuming to apply. Another problem with it is that it tends to crack if the house settles or moves at all (even with the small adjustments which occur as green lumber dries). Stucco is, however, very durable,

Stucco-like exterior siding system is surfaced with an acrylic-base color coating that is highly flexible. In some situations, this may be applied directly over stucco, concrete, prepared masonry, or another approved substrate. Product design: Dryvit Systems.

Built-out architectural detailing (such as window and door surrounds and corner quoins) is easy to create with stucco-like siding system. Acrylic-base finish is applied over insulation board, so house gets insulated from the outside. Architect: Tyler Gazecki.

Brick house isn't actually solid brick construction; it is full-brick veneer over wood framing. To give interest, soldier coursing rims transom arch and clerestory windows. Soldier coursing also bands the house. Architect: William Starmer.

even in harsh marine climates, and is highly resistant to fire.

Relatively new stucco-like systems, often referred to as EIFS (Exterior Insulation Finishing Systems), have eliminated some of the problems of stucco application. Using polymer coatings on a base of fiberglass mesh, foam-board insulation, or fibrous cement board sheathing, these systems require only one or two coats, which are sprayed on by a trained technician.

The resulting material is less expensive and very flexible, with much less tendency to crack. Because the color is mixed into the material, painting isn't necessary—and the palette of possible colors is nearly limitless. As a bonus, the types that employ insulation board add to the building's insulation value.

BRICK & STONE VENEERS

Brick and stone have been popular for centuries. Today, however, they're usually used in the form of veneers rather than as solid-wall construction materials. By applying a surface of brick or stone to the outside of a wood-frame wall, builders can get the look of masonry with less labor. And they can use conventional methods for installing insulation, electrical wires, and water pipes in wood-frame walls.

Masonry veneers are thin stones or bricks or cultured synthetics. Stones are usually 1¼ to 4 inches thick; bricks are typically ½ inch to 4 inches thick. They may come as individual units or as panels.

Construction usually involves attaching the bricks or stones to underlayment with short metal strips called *ties*, then mortaring them in place. This work should be handled by experienced contractors.

In relation to other siding materials, brick and stone are the most expensive options.

True to it's original 1920s style, exterior walls of this remodeled home were sandblasted, then recoated with stucco; pale pink tones are from mixing pink and white color into the stucco. Subtle green roof is random-stagger asphalt-fiberglass shingles that simulate shakes. Architect: Joseph Cristilli, Galvin/Cristilli Architects.

Cotswold-cottage-style stucco wall treatment (above) incorporates rocks, hand-troweled textures, and sandblasted posts and beams. To achieve the amazingly authentic-looking effect, the walls were redone many times. Design: Susan Clark. Realistic stone veneer around base of log-style house (at left) is actually molded aggregate that's lighter than real stone. Each piece is flat on the back and applied individually. Product design: Flying B Stone Co.

Buyer's Guide to Siding Materials

Material	Types and characteristics	Durability
Solid boards	■ Available in many species; redwood and cedar resist decay. Milled in various patterns. See pages 102–103 ■ Nominal dimensions are 1" thick, 4"–12" wide, random lengths to 20'. Bevel patterns are slightly thinner; battens may be narrower ■ Sold untreated, treated with water repellent, primed, painted, or stained ■ Applied horizontally, vertically, or diagonally.	30 years to life of building, depending on maintenance.
Exterior plywood	■ Most siding species are Douglas fir, Western red cedar, redwood, and Southern pine. Face veneer determines designation. Broad range of textures. Typical pattern has grooves cut vertically to simulate solid board siding ■ Sheets are 4' wide, 8'–10' long. Lap boards are 6"–12" wide, 16' long. Thicknesses of both are ⅜"–⅝" ■ Applied vertically or horizontally.	30 years to life of building, depending on maintenance.
Hardboard and OSB	■ Available smooth or textured—rough-sawn, board, stucco, others ■ Sheets are 4' wide, 8'–10' long. Lap boards are 6"–12" wide, 16' long, ⅜"–⅝" thick ■ Sold untreated, treated with water repellent, or opaque stained ■ Sheets are usually applied vertically.	30 years to life of building, depending on maintenance. Prepainted finish guaranteed to 20 years.
Shingles and shakes	■ Mostly Western red cedar, some white cedar. Shingles are graded: #1 ("blue label") are best; #2 ("red label") are acceptable as underlayment when double-coursing. Also available in specialty patterns. Shakes in four shapes and textures, varied by scoring, sawing, or splitting. "Sidewall shingles" are specialty products with heavily machine-grooved surfaces ■ Widths are random from 3"–14". Lengths are 16" (shingles only), 18", and 24". Shakes are thicker than shingles, with butts from ⅜"–¾" thick. Shingles and shakes come prebonded on 8' plywood panels ■ Primarily sold unpainted. Also available prestained, painted, pressure-treated with fire retardant or preservative.	20 to 40 years, depending on heat, humidity, and maintenance.
Vinyl	■ Extruded from polyvinyl chloride (PVC) in white and light colors. Smooth and wood-grain textures are typical. Horizontal panels simulate lap boards. Vertical panels simulate boards with battens ■ Standard length is 12'6".	40 years to life of building.
Aluminum	■ Extruded panels in a wide range of factory-baked colors, textures ■ Types and dimensions are the same as vinyl. Also sold as 12"-by-36" or 12"-by-48" panels of simulated cedar shakes.	40 years to life of building.
Steel	■ Extruded panels in a wide range of factory-baked colors, smooth and wood-grain textures ■ Types and dimensions are the same as vinyl.	40 years to life of building.
Brick and stone veneers	■ Thin bricks or stones or cultured synthetic masonry materials from ½"–4" thick ■ Sold in individual units or panelized ■ Applied over wood framing.	Life of building.
Stucco systems	■ Traditional compound made from fine sand, Portland cement, hydrated lime, and water ■ Applied wet over wire lath in two or three coats. Pigment added to final coat or surface can be painted when dry. Newer polymers are sprayed onto foam- or fiber-cement board sheathing.	Life of building.

It's important to pick a material that wears well both aesthetically and practically. The chart below, with pages 29–45, can help you choose the right material. All siding materials should hold up for a minimum of 20 years when properly maintained. For more about repair and maintenance, see page 114. The relative cost of a particular siding varies from region to region. The only accurate way to estimate is to take basic measurements, figure the square footage that will need coverage (see page 95), and ask a few suppliers or installers for price quotes. Include any sheathing, flashing, furring, or other materials needed.

Maintenance	Installation	Merits and drawbacks
Before using, seal all edges with water-repellent. Needs painting every 4–6 years, transparent staining every 3–5 years, or finishing with water repellent every 2 years.	Difficulty varies with pattern. Most are manageable with basic carpentry skills and tools.	■ Merits: Natural material. Many styles and patterns. Easy to handle and work. Accepts a wide variety of finishes. ■ Drawbacks: Burns. Prone to split, crack, warp, peel (if painted). Species other than cedar and redwood must be finished to protect from termites and rot.
Before using, seal all edges with water repellent, stain sealer, or exterior house paint primer. Restain or repaint every 5 years.	Sheets go up quickly. Manageable with basic carpentry skills and tools.	■ Merits: Can serve as sheathing and siding, adding great structural support to a wall. Many styles, patterns. ■ Drawbacks: Burns. May "check" (show small surface cracks). Susceptible to termite damage when in direct contact with soil, and to water rot if not properly finished.
Before using, seal all edges with water repellent, stain sealer, or exterior house paint primer. Paint or stain unprimed and preprimed hardboard within 60 days of installation; then repeat every 5 years.	Sheets go up quickly. Manageable with basic carpentry skills and tools.	■ Merits: Uniform appearance, without defects typical of wood. Many textures, designs. Accepts finishes well. ■ Drawbacks: Lacks plywood's strength. Susceptible to termite damage when in direct contact with soil, and to water rot and buckling if not properly finished. Cannot take transparent finishes.
In hot, humid climates, apply fungicide/mildew retardant every 3 years. In dry climates, preserve resiliency with oil finish every 5 years.	Time-consuming because of small pieces, but manageable with basic carpentry skills and tools plus a roofer's hatchet.	■ Merits: Rustic wood appearance. Provides small measure of insulation. Easy to handle and work. Easy to repair. Adapts well to rounded walls and intricate architectural styles. ■ Drawbacks: Burns. Prone to rot, splinter, crack, and cup. May be pried loose by wind. Changes color with age unless treated.
Hose off annually.	Manageable with basic carpentry skills and tools, plus a a few specialty tools.	■ Merits: Won't rot, rust, peel, or blister. Burns, but won't feed flames. Easiest synthetic to apply, repair. Resists denting. Scratches do not show. ■ Drawbacks: Light colors only. Sun may cause long-range fading. Brittle when cold.
Hose off annually. Clean surface stains with nonabrasive detergent. Refinish with paint recommended by the manufacturer.	Manageable with basic carpentry skills and tools, plus a a few specialty tools.	■ Merits: Won't rot, rust, or blister. Fireproof. Impervious to termites. Lightweight and easy to handle. ■ Drawbacks: Dents, scratches easily. May corrode near salt water.
Hose off annually. Paint scratches to prevent rust.	Best left to professionals.	■ Merits: Won't rot or blister. Fireproof. Impervious to termites. Resists denting. ■ Drawbacks: Difficult to handle, cut. Rusts if scratched.
Hose off annually.	Professionals only.	■ Merits: Fireproof, durable, and very solid. ■ Drawbacks: Needs professional installation. Expensive.
Hose off annually. If painted, repaint as required.	Professionals only.	■ Merits: Fireproof, durable, solid, and seamless. Can be any color. ■ Drawbacks: Needs professional installation. Expensive. Real stucco can crack with building movement.

GETTING STARTED

Heavy roofing felt is rolled out on solid plywood deck in preparation for concrete-tile roofing. Choosing the right deck and underlayment in relation to the surface material is critical to a successful roofing job.

Whether you're crowning your home with a new roof, giving it a facelift with new siding, or just handling a few exterior repairs, the key to a successful project is careful planning.

Start by assessing what really needs to be done. Will one last patch do for now, or is it really time to reroof or re-side the house? In order to make an informal decision, you'll have to perform a thorough inspection; the following pages will guide you.

Next, determine who will do the work. With an understanding of basic roofing and siding techniques and an idea of the materials involved (see pages 8–47), decide whether you'll be able to do the repair or installation yourself or whether you'll want to hire a professional. This chapter will help you find a competent contractor and prepare a contract that will form the basis for a successful working relationship. You'll also learn about building codes, insurance, and related concerns.

REROOF, RE-SIDE, OR REPAIR?

With the proper repair and maintenance, you may be able to stretch the life of your roofing or siding by a few years, saving—or at least postponing—the cost of a new roof or new siding.

It's a good idea to inspect your roof or siding in autumn, before hard weather hits, then reexamine it again in spring. If you discover problems, make the appropriate repairs, as described on pages 88–93 and 114–125. If this list seems extensive, it may be time for complete replacement.

START IN THE ATTIC

Begin your roof inspection from underneath it, with a visit to the attic. Take along a strong flashlight, a thin screwdriver, a pocketknife, a piece of chalk, and a hammer and some nails or a few short pieces of wire.

To evaluate your roof's general condition, examine the ridge beam, rafters, and sheathing for water stains and dark-colored areas of wet or moist wood. Probe any wet-looking spots with the screwdriver or knife, feeling for softness that may indicate dry rot, and mark them with chalk so you can find them easily later on. Avoid contact with any exposed wiring.

If you must remove fiberglass insulation batts to examine sheathing, wear gloves, goggles, and a dust mask.

If you see pinholes of light that reveal leaks, tap nails or poke wire through them so they'll be visible from the roof's surface. Not every ray of light is a leak. In a wood-shingle roof, small, angled shafts of light that show up in dry weather may be from cracks that swell shut when wet.

If drips are coming through the ceiling, bring a rag and a container to catch the water. Look for dampness on top of ceiling insulation or pooled water on the top side of the ceiling. Try to trace it to its source: often a drip comes from far away, traveling along rafters or sheathing. Peel back insulation, mop up any moisture with the rag, and catch the drips in the container until you can fix the leak.

THEN LOOK FROM OUTSIDE

When you examine the roof from outdoors, you can evaluate the condition of its surface material, flashing, eaves, and gutters.

To check the roof's surface, climb up and take a look (but be sure to read the safety tips on page 51 first) or inspect it from a ladder, using a pair of binoculars. If the roof is tile, concrete tile, or metal, don't walk on it unless you know the material can handle foot traffic. And no matter what the existing surface is, don't walk on it any more than is necessary; you could easily cause more damage.

If you can climb on the roof, take along a pocketknife and screwdriver. Inspect the flashings for any rust spots and for broken seals along the edges. If you have metal gutters and downspouts, look for rust spots and holes.

Use your knife and screwdriver to test the boards along the eaves and rakes (if you don't want to go near the roof's edges, do this from a ladder). To repair these, scrape out any damage caused by dry rot, apply a wood preservative, and fill the holes with wood putty. If the damage is extensive, you can replace boards and finish them to match the existing trim.

Examine the roof for signs of wear, loose or broken nails, or curled, broken, or missing shingles. If you have a sloped roof, check its south side carefully—a southern exposure receives the full force of the sun's rays.

Signs of aging or deterioration in a roof surface vary with the material.

Asphalt shingles may show bald spots where the mineral granules have worn away; large bare patches indicate the roof is beyond its serviceable age. Look for curled shingles, gaps where the wind may have torn shingles away, and cracks in shingle tabs and in ridge and hip shingles.

Pinch a small corner off one or two shingles. If the core appears black, the shingles still have protective oils in them. But if they appear gray and bloated, and if the material crumbles easily between your fingers, they will absorb rather than shed water—and it's probably time for a new roof.

One more test for asphalt shingles: on a reasonably warm day, bend back the ends of several and press them with your fingernail. If they're brittle, they should be replaced.

LOCATING A LEAK

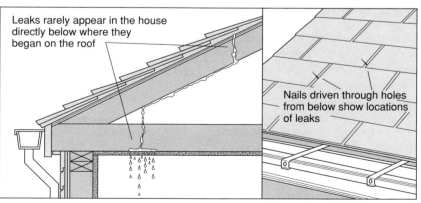

Leaks rarely appear in the house directly below where they began on the roof

Nails driven through holes from below show locations of leaks

Wood shingles can warp or wear thin and become brittle with age. Look for curled, broken, loose, or split shingles, and for spots where nails have become exposed.

Wood shakes show their age when the wood crumbles easily underfoot or between your fingers. Although thick and durable, shakes still grow thin under constant exposure and may split, break, or loosen.

Tile, slate, and other masonry roofing materials are durable, though individual components do chip and break, requiring replacement. To check the felt underlayment, which may give out and need to be replaced, remove a few tiles from several locations on the roof. If the underlayment is black and resilient to the touch, it's still good. If it's gray, swollen, and crumbles easily, it probably needs to be replaced. In that case, the tile or slate must be removed so the underlayment can be replaced but can be put back later.

Metal roofing rarely needs to be replaced for rain failure. More likely problems may be corrosion and dents. For help on repairing and maintaining metal roofs, see page 92.

Low-pitched roofs are difficult to diagnose. Generally, if an almost-flat roof is badly worn, it will announce its condition by leaking. If yours leaks, contact a qualified contractor.

INSPECTING YOUR SIDING

A thorough siding inspection involves looking for obvious problems such as warped boards, missing or damaged shingles, holes in stucco, crumbling mortar, cracks, and defective paint. Don't ignore interior problems such as dry rot and termite damage; these can eventually destroy your house.

Begin with a visual inspection: the drawing shows likely trouble spots. Here are some more detailed observations:

Deteriorated caulking. Make a note of any caulking that has dried out, and renew the seals (page 85). Check the seals around windows and doors; around any plumbing, millwork, or other protrusions; and where a deck or masonry fireplace adjoins a house wall. Caulk any cracks in board siding.

Defective paint. If you find minor problems such as peeling, cracking, scaling, bubbling, or flaking, see page 124–125 for painting tips. If repairs are required, do them first. You can repaint or restain the siding later.

Mildew. Combined heat and humidity can encourage mildew to develop on wood and painted surfaces; it may show up as a fungus-like discoloration or as whitish or moldy deposits. Mildew should be treated with an approved mildewcide.

Efflorescence. Brick or stone veneer may become covered with a white powder called efflorescence, formed when water-soluble salts are washed to the surface. In an old wall, this may be the result of a leak that should be fixed.

Dry rot and termite damage. Dry rot is a fungus that causes wood to crumble; termites destroy wood by chewing out its interior. Both can work away at wood timbers and siding in a way that might easily escape your notice.

To detect damage, probe the edges of wood siding with a knife and look for soft, spongy spots. Pay special attention to any area that's near or in contact with the ground.

To check for visible traces of termites, look for the translucent ½-inch-long wings they grow and shed or the mud tubes some types build. If you find evidence of dry rot or termites, consult a licensed termite inspector or pest control professional.

TYPICAL SIDING PROBLEMS

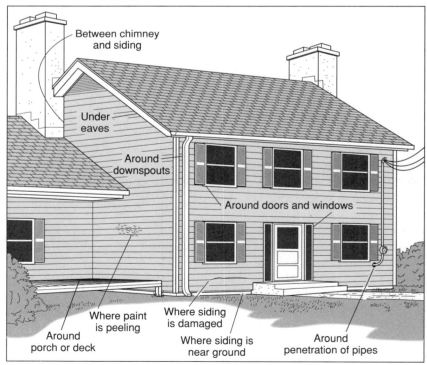

Between chimney and siding

Under eaves

Around downspouts

Around doors and windows

Where paint is peeling

Around porch or deck

Where siding is damaged

Where siding is near ground

Around penetration of pipes

The Height of Safety

Before venturing up a ladder to repair or install roofing or siding materials, be sure you understand these safety basics.

Ladder Safety

Ladders for long reaches range from the straight wooden types to aluminum extension ladders (one that will extend to 20 feet is adequate for most houses). Be sure your ladder is strong, yet light enough to be handled easily.

Here are some tips for using a ladder safely:

■ Inspect your ladder carefully for cracks or weaknesses before you lean it against the house.

■ Set the base of the ladder on firm, level ground, the appropriate distance from the side of the house.

■ Get on and off the ladder by stepping onto the center of the bottom rung. As you climb, use both hands to grip the rails (not the rungs). If the ladder wobbles, back down and reposition it.

■ Keep your hips between the ladder rails. Don't lean out to extend your reach; instead, reposition the ladder.

■ Make sure that only one person stands on a ladder at a time.

■ Install rubber safety shoes (available at home-improvement centers) on the ladder feet if the ladder is to be placed on a slick surface.

■ Don't stand on the top two rungs of a ladder. If using the ladder to gain access to a roof, at least two rungs should extend above the eaves so you can step directly onto the roof.

■ Be sure the rung hooks on an extension ladder are locked in place, and do not extend any one section of the ladder more than three-quarters of its length.

Roof Safety

Let a professional repair any steeply pitched roof—one that slopes more than 25 degrees or rises more than 6 inches vertically for every 12 horizontal inches (a 6-in-12 pitch).

Otherwise, if you've decided to inspect or work on your own roof, remember that any sloped surface is tricky to walk on and can be slick underfoot. Be sure to observe these precautions:

■ Work on the roof only in dry, calm, warm weather. A wet roof can be treacherous, and a sudden wind can knock you off balance. Never

ROOFING BRACKETS

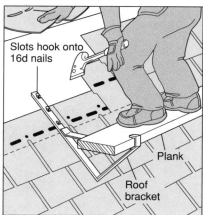

Slots hook onto 16d nails

Plank

Roof bracket

get on the roof when lightning threatens.

■ Wear comfortable clothing and clean, dry, rubber-soled shoes with good ankle support.

■ Keep children and pets away from the work area.

■ Don't walk around on the roof any more than is absolutely necessary, or you could cause more damage. On tile or slate roofs, be extremely cautious: they're slippery and breakable.

■ Be careful not to put your weight on old or brittle roofing materials or rotted decking.

■ Stay well away from power lines; be sure neither your body nor your equipment has contact with them.

Special Safety Equipment

These devices can help to distribute your weight evenly and provide secure footing when you're working on a roof. You may be able to rent them from a tool rental company.

■ A metal ladder bracket allows you to hook a second ladder over the ridge, an aid in moving up and down the roof.

■ Roofing brackets, fastened to the roof framing with 16-penny nails, support planks on which you can work or set your materials. The brackets have notches in them so they can be slipped off the nails after you've shingled over them. Hammer nails flat through the shingles (being careful not to damage shingles).

THE TOOLS & TALENTS IT TAKES

There's hardly a home-improvement project that, successfully done, doesn't offer both tangible and intangible rewards—and roofing and siding are no exceptions. Aside from the pleasure of knowing you did the work yourself, you are also rewarded financially by big savings in labor.

Labor represents about half the cost of a typical roofing or siding project. But while the idea of getting a new roof at half price is pretty appealing, roofing is characteristically a hot, tiring, repetitious job that presents some significant hazards. Siding can also be tedious, heavy, and hazardous.

At the outset, you must make a realistic decision about whether or not you are willing and physically able to see the project through.

DO YOU QUALIFY?

If you want to take on the labor, you should be a careful worker who is competent with tools, adept at following instructions, and able, if necessary, to adapt instructions to the eccentricities of your own house.

You should also be in good physical condition. Kneeling over a slope all day to nail shingles in their courses will tax both your endurance and your back, not to mention the arm and shoulder that must drive all those nails. And whether you're roofing or siding your house, you'll be scooting up and down a ladder and working high up; if you're at all bothered by heights, you're better off turning the project over to a professional.

If you live in a large house, or a tall one perched on a hillside, or one with a steep or complicated roof, strongly consider hiring a contractor to install roofing or siding, unless the area to be worked on is very small.

It's also best to hire a professional if the roof will need structural bracing

ROOFING & SIDING TOOLS

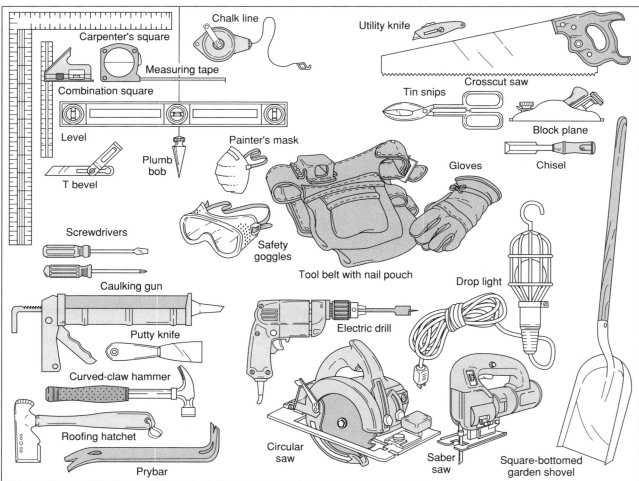

Carpenter's square
Chalk line
Utility knife
Measuring tape
Combination square
Crosscut saw
Level
Tin snips
Plumb bob
Painter's mask
Block plane
T bevel
Gloves
Chisel
Screwdrivers
Safety goggles
Tool belt with nail pouch
Drop light
Caulking gun
Putty knife
Electric drill
Curved-claw hammer
Roofing hatchet
Circular saw
Saber saw
Square-bottomed garden shovel
Prybar

or if the product you choose is particularly heavy or tricky to install. For roofing, such products include tile, slate, concrete tile, some types of metal shingles, standing-seam sheet-metal roofing, and materials for all types of low-slope or flat roofs. Siding products best left to professionals include some vinyl and metal products, stucco (and related systems), and brick and stone veneers.

If you're not sure what will be involved in the work, pick up some of the free instructional brochures manufacturers make available at home-improvement centers.

TOOLS YOU'LL NEED

When you're weighing the idea of doing your own work, your decision will partly be based on what tools you have, what you are willing to buy or rent, and your familiarity with how to use them.

The facing page shows a sampling of the equipment needed for roofing and siding. Be prepared to acquire other tools as more specialized

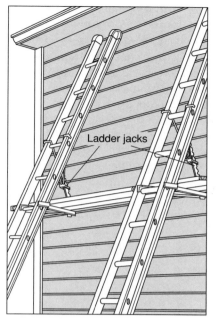

Ladder jacks mount on the inside or outside of a ladder to hold scaffolding.

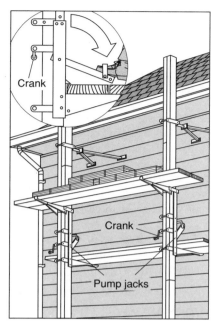

Pump jacks climb doubled 2-by-4 supports; they're operated by a foot pump and crank.

MECHANICAL LIFT

needs arise. You'll also need at least one good ladder—a sturdy, lightweight, 20-foot extension type. Depending on your project, you may want to rent scaffolding, pump jacks, ladder jacks, or a hand-operated lift (shown at left and above).

Also, look into pneumatic nailers or staplers—these can greatly speed up tedious nailing of sheathing and some roofing materials, notably asphalt shingles. For more about these, see page 75.

A roofer's hatchet or claw hammer is the key tool needed for nailing. The roofer's hatchet is best for nailing and aligning wood shingles in their courses and for splitting and scoring wood shingles or shakes. For other types of roofing and for siding, a claw hammer with a smooth face works better.

A utility knife, with extra blades, is used for cutting building paper, roofing felt, and asphalt shingles.

Tin snips are for cutting metal flashings and metal and vinyl trim.

A retractable tape measure, at least 25 feet long, is needed for all measuring tasks.

A chalk line is for snapping visible guides for alignment.

A combination square is needed for marking straight cuts across siding boards and shingles.

A caulking gun is required for applying caulking compound.

A prybar is used for pulling nails and lifting shingles or panels.

A heavy-duty outdoor extension cord is necessary when you're using power tools.

A power circular saw is needed for cutting sheathing, decking, and siding. To cut masonry materials, fit it with a diamond blade.

A power drill and a saber saw are required for making cutouts in wood shingles and siding materials.

A square-bottomed shovel with a short handle makes shingle tear-off easier.

A staple gun is useful for installing insulation, applying building paper to walls, and similar tasks.

A tool belt with loops and pouches is helpful for keeping small tools and nails convenient and accessible.

Gloves protect your hands when working with abrasive materials and sharp flashings.

WORKING WITH PROFESSIONALS

If you decide to turn your project over to a contractor, take as much care in choosing one as you would for any other remodeling project. Ask friends and neighbors for recommendations, and arrange to see some finished work. Get bids and client references from several contractors, then see that a carefully detailed contract is drawn up with the one you select.

Finding and choosing a contractor. Roofs are installed by roofers, listed as "Roofing Contractors" in the telephone directory Yellow Pages. For siding installers, look under "Siding" or "Contractors—Alteration." Vinyl and aluminum siding are also installed by some roofers. You may be able to get referrals from a local branch of the National Roofing Contractors Association (NRCA).

When you call to make your initial contact, be sure the contractor handles your specific type of job and can work within the constraints of your schedule. Boil down your list to two or three candidates. Ask each for a firm bid, based on exactly the same specifications. Also call several former clients of each and ask questions about their experience with quality of workmanship, working relationship, promptness, and readiness to follow up on problems.

Be sure your final candidates are licensed, bonded, and insured for worker's compensation, public liability, and property damage. Also try to determine how financially solvent they are (you can call their bank and credit references). Avoid contractors who are operating hand-to-mouth.

You can request a "performance bond" from some contractors. This guarantees that the work will be finished by him or her. If it isn't, the bonding company will cover the cost of hiring another contractor to complete it. A bond will cost from 2 to 6 percent of the value of your project.

The contractor with the lowest bid will not necessarily be your best bet; quality is critical. Look for a reasonable bid from a contractor with excellent credentials and references.

Drafting a contract. The contract binds and protects both you and your contractor. It sets forth the expectations of both parties. You can minimize the possibility of misunderstandings later by covering every possible contingency here.

The contract should clearly describe all work to be done, specify the materials to be used, and outline both a work schedule and a payment schedule, as discussed below.

■*The project and the participants.* Include a general description of the project, its address, and the names and addresses of both yourself and the contractor.

■*Construction materials.* Identify all materials by brand name, weight, and quality markings. If underlayment, flashing, and gutters are included in the price of the new roof, they should be listed in the contract. Avoid the phrase "or equal," which allows the contractor to substitute materials for your choices.

■*Time schedule.* Though a contractor cannot be responsible for delays caused by strikes and material shortages, he or she should assume responsibility for completing the project within a reasonable period of time. The contract should include both start and completion dates and state that work will be continuous. Most roofing contracts allow about 30 days for completion.

■*Work to be performed.* All work you expect the contractor to do should be clearly defined in the contract. Be clear about who will obtain permits, handle any demolition or tear-off, remove refuse, install insulation, supply fascias or gutters, and so forth.

■*Method of payment.* The contract should also specify how payments are to be made. Typically, a small down payment is made at the outset and remaining payments are due upon delivery and completion. Withhold final payment until the job passes its final inspection and is cleared of all liens. Never pay the full amount until the job is done to your satisfaction.

■*Waiver of liens.* If subcontractors are not paid for materials or services delivered to your home, in some states they can place a "mechanic's lien" on your property, tying up the title. To protect yourself against this possibility, have the general contractor sign a waiver of liens. Licensed contractors are required by law to carry worker's compensation insurance; get it in writing that yours provides it.

■*Warranties.* In addition to manufacturers' warranties, most installers guarantee their work for several years, so make sure this and other promises—such as replacement of landscaping that could be damaged during the progress of the work—have the contractor's signature behind them. If you intend to install the roof yourself, check to be sure that doing so will not invalidate the materials' manufacturers' warranties.

PLAYING BY THE RULES

A number of restrictions will likely affect your roofing or siding project if you're tackling more than a few simple repairs. Here's a primer of common terms and practices.

Building codes. Generally implemented by the city or county building department, codes set standards for safe, long-lasting construction. Codes specify minimum construction techniques and materials for all building situations. Though they are adopted and enforced locally, most regional codes conform to the standards established by the nationally followed Uniform Building Code, Standard Building Code, or Basic Building Code. In some cases, local codes set more restrictive standards. In regard to roofs and exterior walls, they generally specify:

■ The number of reroofs permitted (usually two) on the same structure. This is normally based on the type of roofing material and the structure's ability to hold the weight of additional materials.

■ Requirements for structural integrity of roof and walls, including types of sheathing and nailing patterns.

■ Types of finish materials that may be used, particularly where fire, earthquakes, and wind are a threat.

■ Minimum insulation and weather protection needed in your locale.

Building permits. Permits are required for major home-improvement projects nearly everywhere. If you work with a contractor, his or her firm should secure all necessary permits; otherwise, you'll have to get them yourself. Most permits involve a fee and require inspection by building officials before work can proceed. Permit fees are generally 1 to 2 percent of the project's estimated value—often calculated on square footage. Your inspector or building department can probably tell you over the phone whether or not a permit is required for your project.

Be sure that you file for the necessary permits. Failing to do so can result in fines or legal action against you. You can even be forced to undo the work already performed. At the very least, your negligence may come back to haunt you when you want to sell your house.

Zoning ordinances. Particular to a given community, zoning ordinances restrict setbacks (how near property lines you may build), lot coverage (what percent of your lot your building may occupy), and building height, and set other conditions that necessarily influence design and building. They may also affect the color or type of materials you put on your house's roof and walls, particularly if you live in an historic area or one that has tight architectural controls. If your plans don't conform to zoning ordinances, you may seek a "variance"—an exception to the rules (but be warned, this legal procedure can consume both money and time). If you can prove that your project won't affect your neighbors negatively, a variance may be issued.

CODE RESTRICTIONS

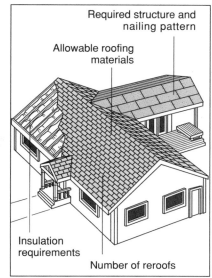

Required structure and nailing pattern

Allowable roofing materials

Insulation requirements

Number of reroofs

OTHER REQUIREMENTS

Check your insurance coverage. Working up on the roof, despite all of your care and precautions, can be dangerous, particularly for amateurs. You'll want to be sure your insurance provides proper medical coverage for yourself, liability coverage for others who volunteer their help, and worker's compensation for any laborers you may hire.

Homeowner's insurance. Because applying new roofing or siding can add significant value to your property, you may want to increase your homeowner's insurance coverage following the improvement. Some policies offer a rate reduction if you've installed fire-resistant materials; ask your insurance agent. For information on the fire ratings of the various roofing materials, see page 26.

Worker's compensation insurance. Though its provisions vary from state to state, worker's compensation insurance generally covers the cost of treatment in case of an occupational injury. It also reimburses the injured worker for wages lost. Many states require it, and contractors are required to carry it for themselves and their employees.

If you will be hiring workers or subcontractors, you can get a worker's compensation policy directly from an insurance company, through an insurance broker, or through a state fund, if your state has one.

Registering as an employer. If you employ people directly and if they will earn more than the minimum amount set by the government, you may be required not only to carry a worker's compensation policy but also to register with the state and federal government as an employer. In this case, you must withhold and remit income taxes and disability insurance and withhold, remit, and contribute to Social Security.

ROOFING PREPARATION

No matter who does the final roofing, several important preparatory tasks must be handled first. These include estimating and ordering materials, preparing the roof deck, installing flashing, and providing ventilation. If you're planning to roof the house yourself, you must handle these steps before you can proceed. If you're hiring a roofer, that person should take care of these jobs. Even so, it's a good idea to familiarize yourself with the methods and choices involved so you can discuss options intelligently with your contractor and make informed decisions.

On the following pages, these important aspects of roofing preparation are discussed. For example, on page 62, you'll find detailed information to help you decide whether you'll be able to roof over the existing roof. If you're doing the work yourself, you'll learn how to prepare the existing roof to receive a new surface. You'll also find information on adding skylights and insulating both roofs and walls—jobs that are easiest to do at the same time the roofing or siding is being replaced.

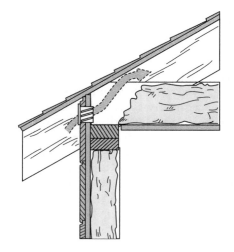

ESTIMATING & ORDERING ROOFING MATERIALS

Before you can order roofing materials, you need to figure how much to order. Estimating is easy if you have a simple roof with unbroken planes—you just calculate the number of squares (one "square" is 100 square feet) your roof's surface comprises.

To do this, first figure the surface area of each of the roof's planes by multiplying the length by the width. Next, total the sums and divide by 100, rounding up to the next whole number (most roofing materials are sold in complete squares only).

For more complex structures and steeper roofs, start by measuring the square footage of the house at ground level. Then, based on the slope of the roof, use the table below to compute the roof's area. For example, suppose you have a house that measures 30 by 40 feet (1,200 square feet) at ground level, and its roof has a 4-in-12 slope.

To compute the roof area, you multiply 1,200 by 1.06—establishing the area here as 1,272 square feet. Divide the roof area by 100, and you get a little less than 13 squares. So you would order 13 squares.

Slope	Multiply by
2 in 12	1.02
3 in 12	1.03
4 in 12	1.06
5 in 12	1.08
6 in 12	1.12
7 in 12	1.16
8 in 12	1.20

Of course, roof shapes are varied. When you estimate your roof surface, adjust for dormers, skylights, chimneys, overlapping roof planes, and overhangs.

If your roof is more complex than you can handle with this information, you're better off leaving the entire job to a contractor.

ESTIMATING

You'll need to estimate your requirements for roofing shingles and felt, hip and ridge shingles (and rake shingles, if you're roofing with masonry or metal), flashing, and nails.

Estimating for shingles and felt. To the number of squares of shingles and felt you estimate you'll need, add 10 percent; this allows for waste, double coverage of shingles or tiles at the eaves, and future small repairs.

Estimating hip and ridge shingles. With asphalt shingles, you can get 100 linear feet of hip and ridge shingles (12-inch squares with 5-inch exposures) from each square. For other materials (such as wood shakes, tile, or metal), measure the lengths of hips and ridges. Then, to determine how many shingles you need, divide the total by the exposure recommended for the material.

Estimating flashings. Measure the lengths of eaves and rakes for drip edge flashings and the lengths of valleys for valley flashing. Vent pipe flashing is sold by the unit—count the number and note the size. Measure the outside dimensions of chimneys and determine the chimney flashing pattern before ordering materials. Figure step flashing and continuous flashing needs for dormers and roof-to-wall connections. For more information, see page 64.

Estimating nails. The number and type of nails you'll need will depend on the roofing material you plan to

apply and the structure of the roof deck—figure 2½ pounds of nails per square of asphalt shingles, 2 pounds per square of wood shingles or shakes or tile. (For other products, follow the manufacturer's recommendations.) You'll also need about 2 pounds of nails for the starter course and for hip and ridge shingles. For miscellaneous sealing, also buy 1 gallon of plastic roofing cement for every 750 square feet of roofing.

WHEN YOU ORDER

Call several roofing suppliers to compare materials costs and delivery charges before you order. To save yourself some backbreaking labor, have materials delivered directly onto the roof after the old surface has been removed—just before it's time to install them. It's important to keep some plastic sheeting on hand to protect exposed decking if delivery is delayed.

Storing materials. If materials will be on the site for an extended period, store them indoors in a dry place, protected from extreme temperatures. If you must leave them outdoors, stack materials off the ground on 2 by 4s and cover them with plastic sheeting to shield them from rain or moisture.

Loading materials. If you must load your own materials onto the roof, either rent a mechanical hoist from a tool supply company or raise materials using a rope strung through a pulley rigged to a ladder (being very careful). Or rent a pulley system at a roofing supply company; this type of rig will work with asphalt, wood, and some lightweight metal products. To use this method, you need to have a helper on the ground to slipknot the rope around each bundle and send it up the ladder.

When you have all the materials up on the roof, scatter the bundles along the ridge to distribute the weight evenly.

PREPARING THE ROOF DECK

To offer years of trouble-free service, a roof requires a proper, sound deck—the part of a roof, consisting of sheathing and underlayment, that supports the finish roofing. Sometimes you can roof right over the old roof, using it as a deck as discussed on page 62. But if your roof doesn't meet the conditions outlined there, you will have to strip the old shingles to get down to a suitable deck or completely remove and replace the decking.

Your new roofing material will dictate what type of deck is best. For most materials, the manufacturer's recommendations and local codes specify the appropriate underlayment, sheathing, flashing, and so forth. The drawings and chart on page 60 illustrate typical practices.

While preparing the deck, you should handle all related changes to the roof, such as adding skylights, vents, or insulation.

TEARING OFF THE OLD ROOF

Removing existing roofing is a particularly dirty, dangerous job. Though you can save money by doing this work yourself, it's often well worth the price to hire a service to strip the roof and remove the debris (look under "Demolition Contractors" in the Yellow Pages).

If you do this work yourself, be very careful. Wear a dust mask to screen out some of the airborne particles, and protect your hands with heavy-duty gloves. Keep your weight on top of the rafters; if you step on weakened or damaged sheathing, you could go right through.

Protect windows and doors below by leaning sheets of plywood against them. To keep debris from flying down onto your flower beds, wrap the upper ends of 6-mil plastic sheeting around 2 by 4s and tack these underneath the eaves, then anchor the sheeting to the ground with a board or other weight.

Plan to rent a large refuse bin from your garbage collection service for the discarded materials, and park it as close to the work site as possible.

If there are two or three existing roofs, remove all of them, one at a time. Be careful not to damage any flashing; even if it has deteriorated and must be replaced, it's useful as a pattern for fabricating new flashing.

When the old shingles have been removed, pull nails and, if necessary, repair damaged sheathing or install new sheathing.

SELECTING SHEATHING

Every roof has either solid or open sheathing across the rafters to provide a nailing base and—in most cases—add to the roof's structural integrity.

Solid sheathing materials come in two forms: panels and boards. Panels, typically 4- by 8-foot sheets of CDX-grade plywood or a pressed-wood product called oriented strand board (OSB), are preferred for most roofs because they're relatively inexpensive and fast to install. Plywood and OSB panels are equally strong; plywood, a little friendlier to handle, is slightly more expensive.

Some older roofs have sheathing made from boards—usually 1 by 6s—butted together; but this construction practice all but disappeared with the availability of less expensive, stronger panel products. Most board sheathing used today is in roofs above cathedral ceilings, where sheathing can be seen from the room below; it typically consists of 1½-inch-thick tongue-and-groove pine

or fir (rigid foam insulation panels are usually applied on top).

Open sheathing, consisting of spaced 1 by 4s or 1 by 6s, is employed only with wood-shingle and shake roofs. The spaces between boards allow air circulation around shingles and shakes, preventing moisture damage from underneath.

INSTALLING PANEL SHEATHING

When installing solid panel sheathing, begin at one lower corner and lay a sheet horizontally across the rafters with its inward edge centered on a rafter, as shown at the top of the facing page. Work your way across the eaves, then lay another full course with the end joints staggered by 4 feet. Leave a ¹⁄₁₆-inch expansion space between the ends of adjoining panels and a ⅛-inch gap between the long sides. In exceptionally humid climates, double this spacing.

If your house has open overhangs, you may want to install starter boards before the first course of panels. Starter board—⅝-inch by 6-inch V-rustic or shiplap siding—is much more attractive to look at from under overhangs than plywood or OSB. When installing starter boards, first snap chalk lines along the eaves as guides for aligning their edges. Join the boards' ends over rafters.

You can install ⅜-inch panel sheathing over the top of existing open sheathing, but the roof will have more structural integrity if you remove the open sheathing and start from scratch with thicker panels. For a standard roof with rafters on 24-inch centers, choose ½-inch-thick plywood or OSB sheathing.

When standard ½-inch panels are used, it's usually necessary to support them mid-span between rafters, either with blocking or with special H-clips that serve to keep panels flush. Or buy plywood panels with interlocking V-grooved edges.

PLYWOOD SHEATHING

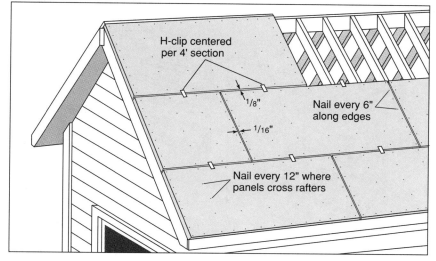

H-clip centered per 4' section

1/8"

1/16"

Nail every 6" along edges

Nail every 12" where panels cross rafters

TONGUE-AND-GROOVE SHEATHING

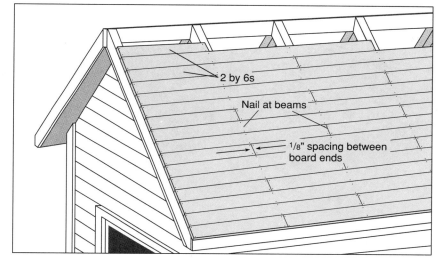

2 by 6s

Nail at beams

1/8" spacing between board ends

OPEN SHEATHING

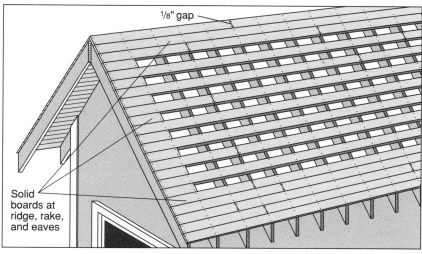

1/8" gap

Solid boards at ridge, rake, and eaves

Nail panels to rafters with 8-penny galvanized common nails, spaced every 6 inches along the vertical ends of each panel and every 12 inches along intermediate rafters. Align panel edges with the centers of rafters, offsetting ends of panels for each course by 4 feet.

Let panels extend over hips and ridges. Snap a chalk line across them flush at rakes, hips, and ridge, and cut them off in place (be very careful not to put your weight on unsupported ends).

INSTALLING TONGUE-AND-GROOVE BOARD SHEATHING

Choose well-seasoned boards in lengths of 4-foot multiples so you can join them where they cross beams; stagger the joints. Tongue-and-groove joints should fit snugly together but allow ⅛-inch expansion space where board ends meet. Use 8-penny galvanized common nails for nailing ¾-inch lumber and 16-penny nails for 1½-inch lumber. Fasten each board, turned best side down, with two nails wherever it crosses a beam, as shown in the drawing at center left.

INSTALLING OPEN SHEATHING

Open sheathing consists of well-seasoned 1 by 4s spaced center to center a distance equal to a shingle's or a shake's exposure, or 1 by 6s spaced center to center a distance equal to twice the exposure. Fasten each board to the rafters with two 8-penny galvanized common nails, allowing ⅛ inch as expansion space where boards meet end to end as shown in the drawing at bottom left.

At overhangs, sheathing should be continuous—without gaps. Begin by installing solid rows of 1 by 4s at the eaves and rakes, as shown. If these areas are visible from below, place the best side of the sheathing downward. Run the decking solid for the last 18 inches at the ridge.

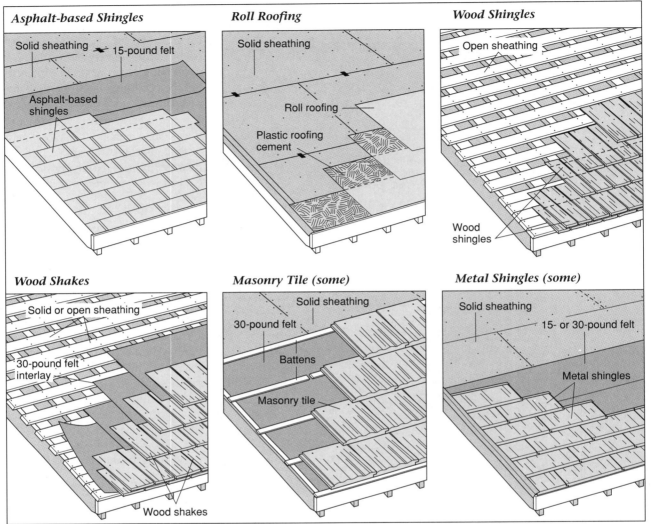

Asphalt-based Shingles

Solid sheathing — 15-pound felt

Asphalt-based shingles

Roll Roofing

Solid sheathing

Roll roofing

Plastic roofing cement

Wood Shingles

Open sheathing

Wood shingles

Wood Shakes

Solid or open sheathing

30-pound felt interlay

Wood shakes

Masonry Tile (some)

Solid sheathing

30-pound felt

Battens

Masonry tile

Metal Shingles (some)

Solid sheathing

15- or 30-pound felt

Metal shingles

ROOF DECK REQUIREMENTS FOR HOMEOWNER-INSTALLED MATERIALS

The finish roofing material selected determines the decking materials to use. As shown below, when roofing over, some materials may be applied directly over old roofs; others may require the installation of battens to provide air circulation.

Finish roofing	*New roof decking*		*Roof-over options* (where codes and conditions permit)
	Sheathing	**Underlayment**	
Asphalt/composition shingles	Solid	15# felt	Asphalt-based shingles, roll roofing, some wood shingles
Roll roofing	Solid	None	Roll roofing
Wood shingles	Open	None	Battens on some asphalt-based shingles
Wood shakes	Solid or open	30# felt interlay	Asphalt-based shingles, roll roofing, wood shingles
Masonry tile	Solid	30# felt (or heavier)	Some asphalt-based shingles, roll roofing; may require battens and additional support
Metal shingles	Solid	15# or 30# felt	Some asphalt-based shingles, roll roofing, wood shingles; may require battens

INSTALLING UNDER- LAYMENT

Roofing felt, a heavy, asphalt-impregnated black paper sold in large rolls, provides a second layer of weather protection beneath many roof surfaces. Two thicknesses are commonly used, 15-pound and 30-pound. On most roofs, strips of standard 36-inch-wide, 15-pound felt are lapped from the eaves to the ridge and are used to line valleys. For wood shake roofs, 18-inch-wide, 30-pound felt is sandwiched between courses of shakes, as shown on page 60. Wood shingles and roll roofing are applied without underlayment.

Applying drip edges. Before you install underlayment, install metal drip edges along the eaves and valley liners and flashing (see page 64). After underlayment is in place, drip edges are applied along the rakes. Refer to page 65 for information on drip-edges and flashings.

Sweep off the roof deck and check for protruding nails or panels not properly nailed, then prepare to roll out the underlayment.

Snapping chalk lines. To align rows of felt underlayment evenly, measure the roof carefully and snap horizontal chalk lines before you begin. Snap the first line 33⅝ inches above the eaves (for a ⅜-inch overhang). Then, providing for a 2-inch overlap between strips of felt (follow the lines printed on most felt), snap each succeeding chalk line at 34 inches.

Nailing on the felt. Start at one end of one of the eaves and work from rake to rake. Tack the felt at its center with three roofing nails and roll a strip to the other end of the eave. Cut it off flush at the rake. Adjust the strip up or down and smooth it out. Nail the material in place with roofing nails spaced 3 to 4 feet apart along the lower half of the felt.

Repeat this process, applying each subsequent strip with a 2-inch overlap and nailing through this lap until you reach the ridge. Trim the felt with a utility knife, flush at rakes and overlapped 6 inches at valleys, hips, and ridges. Where two strips meet end to end, overlap by 4 inches.

When you encounter a vent pipe, slit the felt to fit around the pipe, then continue rolling out the felt. (Mason-ry tile requires special vent flashing as shown on page 82.)

Many low-pitched roofs—those flatter than 4 in 12—require installation of two separate layers of felt over the entire roof; check local codes.

Dealing with ice and snow. To protect an asphalt shingle roof against ice dams, first apply standard underlayment to the sheathing. Then cover the eaves area—to 12 inches inside the exterior-wall line—with a 36-inch-wide sheet of 90-pound mineral-surface or 50-pound smooth-surface roll roofing.

Allowing a ⅜-inch overhang along the eaves, fasten down the roll roofing at intervals of 12 to 18 inches, 6 inches from the bottom edge and 1 inch from the upper edge. At vertical joints, allow 4 inches overlap; fasten the lower lap to the roof with nails every 12 inches, and cement the two ends together as illustrated below.

REINFORCING EAVES

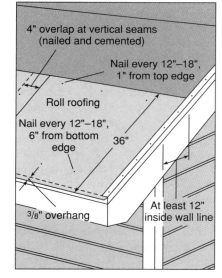

4" overlap at vertical seams (nailed and cemented)

Nail every 12"–18", 1" from top edge

Roll roofing

Nail every 12"–18", 6" from bottom edge

36"

⅜" overhang

At least 12" inside wall line

If you need more than one width of roll roofing to reach 12 inches inside the wall line, overlap horizontal courses by at least 6 inches, applying plastic roofing cement liberally where they overlap. See page 71 for more about dealing with cold climates.

APPLYING UNDERLAYMENT

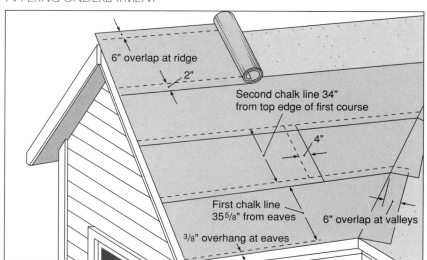

6" overlap at ridge

2"

Second chalk line 34" from top edge of first course

4"

First chalk line 35⅝" from eaves

⅜" overhang at eaves

6" overlap at valleys

ROOFING OVER THE EXISTING ROOF

Using the existing roof as the deck for a new surface is undoubtedly the easiest route to a new roof—it saves you the time and trouble of stripping the old shingles off and provides an extra layer of protection in case rain falls after work is underway.

But whether or not you can roof over the old surface depends on the condition of the present surface and sheathing; the compatibility of old and new surface materials; the number of roofs the framework already supports; the manufacturer's recommendations for your roofing material; and local building codes and requirements. Roofing over certain materials, such as wood shingles, can compromise the new roof's fire safety and lower its rating; to learn more, check with your building department.

In most areas, you're permitted three asphalt-based roofs—the original and two reroofs—or two wood-shingle roofs on the original framework. Your building inspector can tell you what the limits are in your community. Of course, if the rafters are already sagging under the current load, you'll have to strip the roof and start from scratch—and maybe strengthen the framework.

In some cases, you can mix materials, applying one kind of product over another. You can put wood shingles or shakes or some metal or masonry roofing products over asphalt if the framework can handle the weight. And although you can install asphalt or some metal or masonry materials over wood, many professional roofers advise against it because the old shingles, particularly when damp, can trap moisture under the surface, resulting in dry rot and deterioration. When installing some roofing materials, you can solve this problem by nailing battens onto the existing roof to promote ventilation.

Be sure that both the old surface and the sheathing underneath are in good condition. If the sheathing has been badly damaged by water, it will have to be patched or replaced.

Check that the existing shingles lie flat—roofing over curled shingles will give your new roof a lumpy look. If you find that a few shingles are missing, you can replace them before roofing over; but if you find large bare areas, it's best to strip down to the sheathing. You need to be sure you have a uniform, stable nailing base for the new roof.

PREPARING TO ROOF OVER

To prepare the old surface for a new roof, replace missing shingles as necessary and nail down asphalt shingles that have curled, buckled, or split; or nail down curled or warped wood shingles. Strip off ridge and hip shingles, removing nails as you work, so new materials will lie flat. Then sweep the roof clean of debris.

When a roof is roofed over, the old roof is often visible along the eaves and rakes. To hide the old roof completely, use a utility knife (for asphalt) or a hatchet (for wood) to strip away 6 inches of roofing material from the eaves and rakes. Then nail on a 1-by-6 board and add a metal drip edge as described on page 65. Besides camouflaging the old roof, the board provides a firm base for nailing along what is often the weakest part of the old roof, its edges.

Inspect all chimney and vent flashings to be sure they are in good order; if not, replace them. Check, too, to see if mortar on the chimney needs repair.

When reroofing, it's smart—but not required—to apply new roofing felt first (see page 61). Also, install new valley, eaves, and dormer flashings (see page 64).

EAVES & RAKE BUILDUP

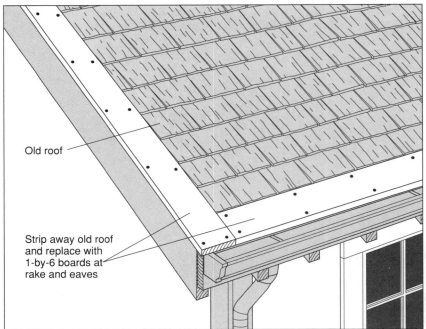

Old roof

Strip away old roof and replace with 1-by-6 boards at rake and eaves

INSTALLING BATTENS

Some kinds of roofing call for battens to be applied either over existing roofing or on new, solid decking. For example, if you're putting wood shingles over existing asphalt shingles, or roofing with some types of tile on top of solid sheathing, battens may be required. Naling down the battens is easy; figuring proper placement can be a little complicated.

Battens for wood shakes or shingles.

When you apply battens over solid sheathing or old shingles, use well-seasoned 1 by 4s. Lay the first board flush with the eaves. From there, space boards so their centers are the same distance apart as the exposure for the shingle—5 inches for a 5-inch exposure, 7½ inches for a 7½-inch exposure, and so on.

Allow ⅛-inch spacing where board ends meet, and extend the boards ½ inch beyond the rake. On each side of the ridge, run two strips side by side to provide more nailing area. In the valleys, leave ½ inch between abutting strips.

Battens for masonry tiles and some metal roofings.

If battens are required for the finish roofing, install 1 by 2s at intervals equal to the exposure of the tile or shingle.

If you're installing flat tiles or shingles, nail a batten flush with the eaves, as shown at right ("birdstop" flashing is nailed at the eaves when curved tiles are installed). Lay sample tiles or shingles along the eaves at each rake, allowing for the recommended overhang—usually 1¼ inches for a roof with gutters, 2 to 3 inches for one without. Mark at both rakes where the lugs of the tile or shingle will grip the upper edge of the batten (from the top of the tile or shingle to the lug grip is usually 1 inch). Then snap a chalk line across the roof between the two marks.

Next, install the battens, placing their upper edges against the chalk line. Fasten them to the roof with 1½-inch galvanized nails wherever they

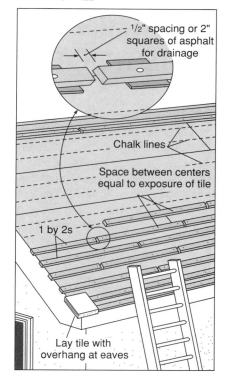

BATTENS: TILE

½" spacing or 2" squares of asphalt for drainage

Chalk lines

Space between centers equal to exposure of tile

1 by 2s

Lay tile with overhang at eaves

cross a rafter. To accommodate water runoff, allow ½-inch spacing between abutting strips. Set a batten at the roof ridge, its upper edge 1 inch (or the distance from the upper border of the tile or shingle to the bottom of the lug) from the top of the ridge.

Then measure the distance between upper edges of the two battens. Divide the distance by the recommended tile exposure. (Measure and calculate twice for accuracy.)

If your calculations yield a multiple of the recommended exposure that's a whole number, simply mark the exposures along each rake, starting from the top edge of the batten near the eaves. Snap horizontal chalk lines from rake to rake, and install battens with their upper edges set against the chalk lines. If the roof doesn't divide into a whole multiple of the exposure, decrease the exposure slightly for all courses. (Always decrease—not increase—exposures to compensate for a roof's irregularities.)

BATTENS: WOOD SHINGLES & SHAKES

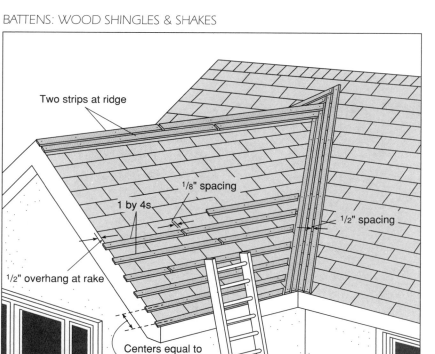

Two strips at ridge

⅛" spacing

1 by 4s

½" spacing

½" overhang at rake

Centers equal to length of shingle or shake exposure

FLASHING THE ROOF

Flashings made of galvanized steel, copper, or aluminum sheet metal serve as impervious barriers. Properly placed, flashings direct water away from places where there are joints in roofing materials—in valleys, around chimneys and vent stacks, where dormers and other walls meet the roof, and along the eaves and rakes.

The flashing materials and methods discussed here are appropriate for most do-it-yourself roofing—using asphalt shingles, wood shingles and shakes, and some masonry and metal products. For instructions on handling variations, check manufacturers' specifications.

Standard flashings—preformed and ready to install, for most applications—are available at home-improvement centers and roofing supply companies. For custom needs, contact a sheet-metal fabricator.

The most common flashings and installation methods follow:

THREE VALLEYS

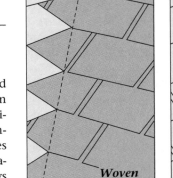

Woven

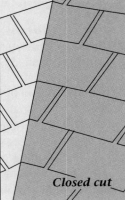

Closed cut

Open

WEAVING A VALLEY

Nail at least 6" from valley center

A CLOSED-CUT VALLEY

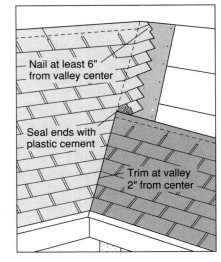

Nail at least 6" from valley center

Seal ends with plastic cement

Trim at valley 2" from center

TYPICAL ROOF FLASHING

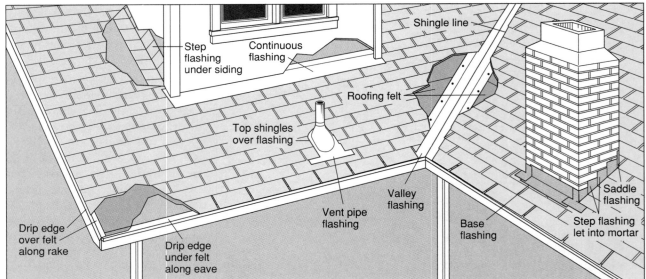

Step flashing under siding

Continuous flashing

Shingle line

Roofing felt

Top shingles over flashing

Vent pipe flashing

Valley flashing

Base flashing

Saddle flashing

Step flashing let into mortar

Drip edge over felt along rake

Drip edge under felt along eave

Valley flashings. Valleys require particularly sturdy flashing because they carry more water off a roof than does any individual roof plane. The most common valley flashing is a W-shaped aluminum or galvanized metal channel that comes in 10-foot lengths and in 16- to 24-inch widths (the lower the roof's pitch, the wider the flashing it requires). Some types have crimped "slater's edges" that help direct water toward the center of the flashing.

On most roofs, metal valley flashing is installed after a felt liner is in place and before the primary underlayment and finish roofing go on.

To install metal valley flashing for an asphalt, shake, or masonry roof, first roll out a length of 15-pound roofing felt cut to the length of the valley. Push it snugly into the valley, and, using roofing nails, nail it every 2 to 4 feet along the outside edges.

If you'll need more than one length of flashing to cover the valley, start at the bottom and overlap the first length with the second one by at least 6 inches. If the valley flashing has slater's edges, fasten the flashing in place with special clips, applied in pairs every 4 feet as shown at right, center. Otherwise, using roofing nails of the same metal as the flashing (galvanized steel for galvanized flashing, aluminum for aluminum flashing, bronze for copper flashing), nail every 6 inches along the flashings' edges. At ridges or where two valleys meet, cut flashings with tin snips so you can overlap them (the upper one over the lower) and nail them down.

On some asphalt-shingle roofs, shingles are woven across the valleys, eliminating the need for metal flashings (as shown on the facing page). This is generally the best way to handle valleys between roof planes of different pitches. Another fairly common technique for asphalt-shingle roofs is to flash valleys with roll roof-

INSTALLING METAL VALLEYS

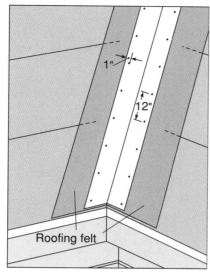

Roofing felt

SLATER'S EDGES & CLIPS

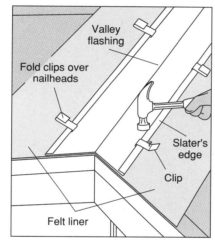

Valley flashing

Fold clips over nailheads

Slater's edge

Clip

Felt liner

ROLL-ROOFING VALLEY

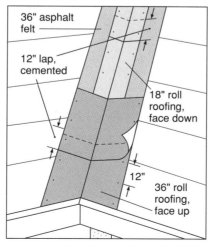

36" asphalt felt

12" lap, cemented

18" roll roofing, face down

12"

36" roll roofing, face up

ing that is the same color as the shingles. To do this, first nail an 18-inch-wide strip along the valley, with the finished surface down; set nails about 1 inch in from the edges and space them at 12-inch intervals. Then roll out a full, 36-inch-wide strip, finished side up, and center it over the first strip; nail it down in the same way.

Drip edges and flashings for eaves. Drip edges keep water from wicking back under the roofing material along eaves and rakes. Along eaves, nail preformed metal drip edges in place before you apply the roofing felt. Fit the drip edges tightly against the fascia board (if there is one) and nail through the top deck surface (not the fascia) at about 10-inch intervals, using roofing nails. Overlap adjoining lengths about 1 inch; cut them flush at the rakes.

After applying the roofing felt, nail drip edges along the rakes, using the same technique.

In climates where ice dams may occur along eaves, flash with a special rubber or plastic ice-shield membrane or roll roofing from the eaves to at least 12 inches beyond the inside wall line. On a cedar-shingle or shake roof, use 30-pound felt for this task—but run it more than 24 inches beyond the inside wall line. (For more about ice dams, see pages 61 and 71.)

INSTALLING DRIP EDGES

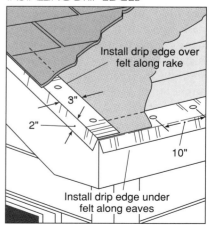

Install drip edge over felt along rake

3"

2"

10"

Install drip edge under felt along eaves

Vent pipe flashings. Before you begin to roof, be sure to have on hand vent pipe flashings to fit each pipe that penetrates the roof. You can buy sheet-metal cone flashings that you caulk to the pipe or self-sealing types that come with rubber sleeves or gaskets.

Vent pipe flashing is installed when the new roofing material has been applied up to the base of the vent pipe. You cut the roofing material to fit around the pipe, slide the flashing over the pipe so that its base flange fits over the roofing material on the down-slope side, then continue roofing over the flashing, cutting the roofing to fit around it.

Some roofers recommend using two wide-skirt (extra-large-flange) flashings on masonry roofs. You apply the first one over the roofing felt and work the other into the masonry tile as the tile is installed.

Chimney flashings. Typically, chimney flashing consists of several parts: solid base flashing along the bottom of the lowest side, overlapping step flashing along ascending sides, and continuous saddle flashing at the base of the uphill side. A second layer, called cap flashing, overlaps the edges of the flashing below it on all sides; this cap is mortared or caulked to the chimney.

You can buy step flashings sized to correspond with the exposure of your roofing material. But unless you can form the base, saddle, and cap flashings yourself, you'll need to have these components made by a sheet-metal fabricator. To form them yourself, cut the pieces from 26-gauge sheet stock as shown and clamp them between 2 by 4s to make straight bends.

The time to flash a chimney is when the new roofing material has been applied up to the chimney's base. If the roof is particularly steep or if the chimney is more than 2 feet wide along its uphill side, it's a good

CHIMNEY FLASHING

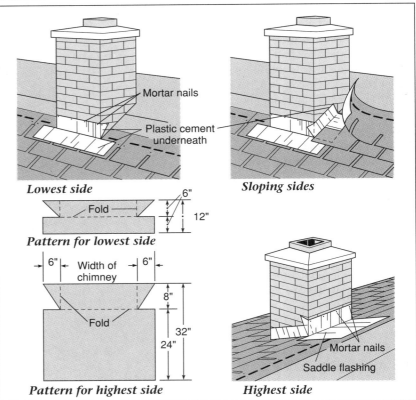

Lowest side

Pattern for lowest side

Pattern for highest side

Sloping sides

Highest side

CRICKET FLASHING

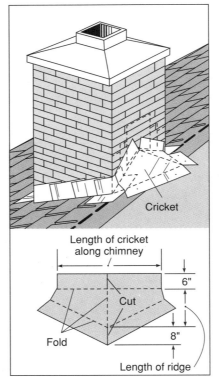

CAP FLASHING

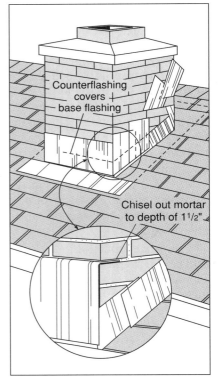

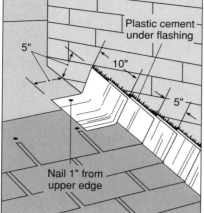

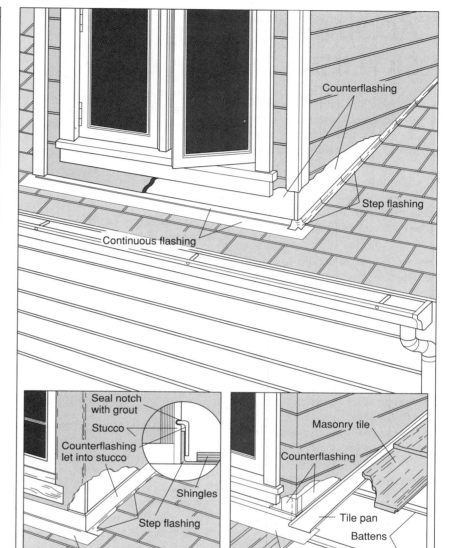

idea to build a "cricket" of two ply-wood triangles (as shown in the drawing on the facing page) so water doesn't collect behind the chimney. Saddle flashing must be designed to fit over this cricket.

Apply asphalt primer, then plastic roofing cement to the bricks where the base flashing goes on the front of the chimney—and put this flashing in place. Work your way up the roof's slope with shingles and step flashing as shown above, embedding both ends of the shingles and step flashings in plastic roofing cement. Shingle to the edge of the cricket, then embed the saddle flashing in plastic roofing cement and nail it to the deck (but nowhere else). Using an old screwdriver, rake mortar from the joints between bricks, set the front and side cap flashings about 1 inch into these spaces, and remortar. Finish by installing cap flashings on rear corners.

Continuous flashings. These protect areas where a sloped roof meets a vertical wall—for example, where a dormer's front wall intersects the roof. How this joint should be flashed depends upon whether or not the wall already has siding on it. The easiest method is to run L-shaped metal flashing (the "L" bent to match the roof's slope) along the

joint before siding has been applied but after finish roofing is in place. If the wall has already been sided, you can install continuous flashing and counterflashing along the joint, as shown above.

Skylight and dormer flashings. Self-flashing skylights (see page 69) have built-in flanges that sit on the roof deck. A skylight mounted on a curb (a wood frame attached to the roof deck) requires flashing like

that for chimneys, installed around all sides.

Dormer side walls are flashed with step flashing, fitted in place as each course of roof shingles goes on (see methods shown above). For the best seal, set each step flashing in a bed of roofing cement, using more roofing cement to fix each shingle to the metal. Ideally, step flashings should be slipped up under the siding; if that's not possible, caulk them to the siding.

ADDING A SKYLIGHT

A skylight can fill a room with natural light, make a space feel expansive, and reduce energy bills, providing warmth from the sun in the winter, and—if it's the ventilating type—promoting air circulation in hot weather. By far the easiest time to install a skylight is when you're reroofing.

Skylights are made of plastic or glass. Lightweight acrylic or polycarbonate skylights are durable and economical; standard models come in many shapes. Glass skylights don't scratch, yield a clearer view, and come in many different sizes and types, with various energy-saving and sun-filtering features.

A skylight is designed for a specific range of roof pitches. For example, fixtures for very low slopes have special curbs, and those for steep slopes have splash guards.

If you understand basic carpentry, installing a fairly small (under 4- by 4-foot) square or rectangular skylight on an asphalt or wood-shingle roof with a moderate slope (to 6 in 12) is manageable. First, check to see whether a building permit is required. And when you buy the fixture, be sure you get the manufacturer's specifications on dimensions for the rough opening as well as installation instructions.

PREPARING THE OPENING

A skylight is easiest to install over a room with a cathedral-style ceiling, where you simply frame an opening to fit it. Otherwise, you must build a light shaft from the skylight to a ceiling opening in the room below.

To plan the ceiling opening, take into account the skylight's size, the light shaft you intend to build, and the roof's slope. You must also plan around existing framing, plumbing, wiring, or other obstructions.

The light shaft's shape determines how light is delivered to the room below. A shaft with splayed sides diffuses light over a wider area than does one with straight sides. The shaft's shape also affects the size of the ceiling opening and its relation to the roof opening (see drawing on the facing page).

Mark the corners of your preferred ceiling hole location by driving nails through the ceiling. If any nails hit solid wood—most likely the ceiling joists—shift the location slightly. Then, from the attic, find these nails. Use a plumb bob, straightedge, framing square, or measuring tape to identify a corresponding location on the underside of the roof, being sure this matches the opening required for the skylight. Drive long nails up through the roofing materials to outline the shape on the roof's surface.

If the skylight is to be mounted on a curb frame, build a curb of 2 by 6s, with inside dimensions the same as those of the rough opening. Use a framing square to be sure the curb's corners are square, then brace them with small triangles made from ½-inch plywood. Set the curb over the four nail points. If the nails don't fall just inside each corner, measure the curb's size again and, if it's right, adjust the roof opening's outline.

For an asphalt or wood-shingle roof, mark the curb's outer perimeter on the roof. Extend these lines 3 inches beyond the top and bottom corners of the curb and mark lines between these points, parallel to the top and bottom of the curb. Remove roofing material from this area (the hole through the sheathing will be smaller). If you have a heavy shake roof, plan to remove an extra ½ inch along each side of the curb.

For a self-flashing skylight (requiring no curb), first check the placement of the four nails by setting the skylight over them. Then mark lines approximately 10 inches beyond the nails along the top and the two sides and 2 inches below the nails along the bottom to designate the area where roofing will be removed.

CUTTING & FRAMING

Don't cut the roof hole until you're sure you have a couple of rain-free days to complete the work. A circular saw with a combination blade is best for cutting through wood shingles or shakes, sheathing, and rafters. (When cutting through shingles or shakes, adjust the blade so it cuts only through the roofing, not the sheathing.) A utility knife may work better for cutting asphalt shingles.

After you've cut the opening, pry the roofing loose, saving shingles for patching around the skylight's perimeter later.

Next, checking your existing framing and referring to the drawing on the facing page, determine how best to frame the opening. The framing should be 1½ inches thick and the same width as rafters. For headers, add an extra 3 inches to the rough opening's dimensions; for rafters and jack rafters, add 1½ inches. Mark cutting lines on the sheathing. Set a circular saw's blade to cut just through the sheathing, then cut the hole.

Before cutting a rafter, support each end of the portion to be removed by nailing a 2 by 4 to the rafter and the ceiling joist below. Leave supports in place until you've installed headers. (Note in the drawing that the angle at which rafters must be cut in order to secure the headers depends on the angle of the light shaft you want.) Nail framing with 16-penny galvanized common nails; mount headers with double joist hangers nailed to rafters. Patch sheathing so it's flush with the rough opening.

SECURING THE SKYLIGHT

The following methods should work for most skylights, but check the directions provided with yours.

If you're installing a curb-mounted unit, toenail the curb to the rafters or jack rafters and to the headers. Pay special attention to the manufacturer's instructions concerning flashing. In most cases, you flash the curb with continuous flashing along the down-roof side, step flashing up both sloped sides, and saddle flashing (similar to that used for a chimney) across the top. Run a wavy bead of caulk around the top of the curb, center the skylight over the curb, and press the fixture firmly into the sealant. Nailing through the predrilled holes, secure the skylight's frame to the side of the curb.

If you're installing a self-flashing unit, set it over the opening and mark the outer edge of the flange on the roof. Remove the fixture and liberally cover the area within the lines with roofing cement. Reposition the skylight, setting it squarely over the opening, press the flange firmly into the cement, and secure it with roofing nails. Generously cover nailheads and the flange with roofing cement. Replace shingles or shakes as needed.

OPENING THE CEILING

Double-check your original ceiling marks against the roof opening and the intended angle of the light shaft. Snap a chalk line between the nails for your cuts. (Before cutting, protect the floor and furniture with a large tarp or drop cloths.) Wearing a dust mask and eye protection, make the required cuts, removing any heavy ceiling material in small pieces.

To cut through wallboard, use a keyhole or reciprocating saw. Cut lath and plaster with a reciprocating saw fitted with a coarse wood-cutting blade. At joists, cut only the surface material—not the joist.

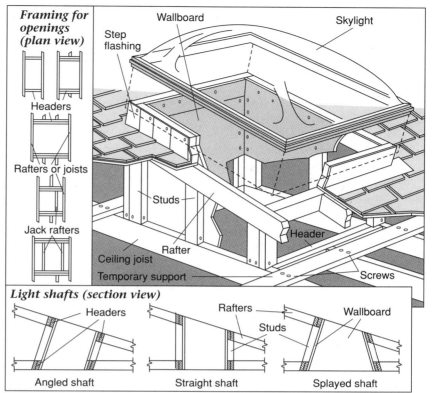

Framing for openings (plan view)
Headers
Rafters or joists
Jack rafters

Step flashing
Wallboard
Skylight
Studs
Header
Rafter
Ceiling joist
Temporary support
Screws

Light shafts (section view)
Headers — Angled shaft
Straight shaft
Rafters
Studs
Wallboard
Splayed shaft

Before cutting a joist, make a temporary support of two 2 by 4s laid flat across the joists to extend at least 12 inches beyond each side of the intended hole; these 2 by 4s should be long enough to span both the opening and two joists on each side of it. Use long wood screws to fasten the 2 by 4s to each joist they cross. Depending on the size of the opening, the rafter and/or ceiling joist at the side of the opening may have to be doubled.

Frame the ceiling opening as you did the roof opening. Cut the ceiling joists, then frame with headers.

BUILDING A LIGHT SHAFT

Frame the light shaft as shown, toenailing studs to ceiling and roof framing with 8-penny nails. Be sure there are two studs at each corner to provide a nailing surface for wallboard.

Staple insulation between the studs in the light shaft. Then cut pieces of ½-inch-thick gypsum wallboard for the shaft's inner walls. To do this, score along your cutting line with a utility knife and break the gypsum core by bending the wallboard toward the back. Score the back paper along the break, then snap the board to sever it cleanly.

Nail wallboard inside the shaft, using drywall nails spaced about 6 inches apart. With the last hammer blow on each nail, dimple the surface of the wallboard slightly, creating a shallow pocket for wallboard compound. Measure and cut four metal corner bead pieces to rim the perimeter of the ceiling hole; nail these in place. Then, following directions provided on the container of wallboard compound, cover the nailheads and tape the joints. For best light reflection, paint the shaft white; otherwise, paint it to match the ceiling.

ROOF VENTILATION

The more airtight you make your house by weather-stripping, caulking, and insulating it, the greater the need for proper ventilation. If your house can't "breathe," unwanted heat, moisture, fumes, and vapors can build up.

Without adequate ventilation through roof vents and attic fans, moisture condenses in the attic and eventually damages sheathing, rafters, insulation—even roofing materials. Vents and fans move fresh air throughout a house, dispelling unwanted air and pollutants.

The time to improve ventilation is when you prepare the roof deck.

HOW MUCH VENTILATION?

As a general rule, provide 1 square foot of free vent (without wire or grillwork) for each 150 square feet of attic floor area. Subtract the area taken up by wire or grillwork. A vent covered with ⅛-inch or ¼-inch wire mesh should be 1¼ times as large as a free vent opening for the same area. A vent covered with ¼-inch wire mesh and a louver will need to be twice as large.

A ratio of 1 square foot of free vent opening for each 300 square feet of attic floor may be adequate if a vapor barrier is installed on the room side of attic insulation and if half of the vent space is near the tops of the gables or along the ridge.

If natural venting is inadequate, an attic fan may be needed to push air through the vents. A building inspector or a ventilation contractor can help you determine whether your house needs additional vents. (You can find contractors by looking in the Yellow Pages under "Contractors, Heating and Ventilating.")

TYPES OF VENTILATION

The illustration below shows typical roof ventilation.

Ridge vents. Because the warmest air collects at the top of the roof, the ridge is a very efficient place for ventilation, using a ridge vent—a long, inverted metal trough that permits air flow out of the house without admitting rain. Install ridge vents before roofing materials are applied.

Gable ventilators. Triangular gable ventilators, made of galvanized metal, are sold at home-improvement centers or sheet-metal shops. Installed at the tops of gables, they dispel heat that rises to the ridge.

Soffit ventilators. Rectangular ventilators placed at the soffit or eaves area of the roof let cool air flow in. Convection then draws warm air up to and out through gable or ridge ventilators. Soffit ventilators help keep roof decks and insulation dry and help eliminate problems caused by ice dams (see facing page).

Roof-plane turbines and fans. Turbine vents placed on the roof plane act as free ventilating space in calm weather, but generate an air flow from turbine action when the wind blows.

Powered attic exhaust fans will augment natural air convection. Placed over ceiling vents, these fans can substantially reduce air-conditioning needs.

A whole-house ventilating fan, installed in the attic floor, cools the entire house by drawing cool air through open windows and vents in rooms below, pulling that air up into the attic, and forcing it out through attic vents.

When purchasing an exhaust fan, consider its air flow in terms of cubic feet per minute (CFM) and its noise level. Fan noise is rated in "sones." The lower the number of sones, the quieter the fan.

To install turbines or fans, consult the manufacturer's instructions.

ROOF VENTILATION

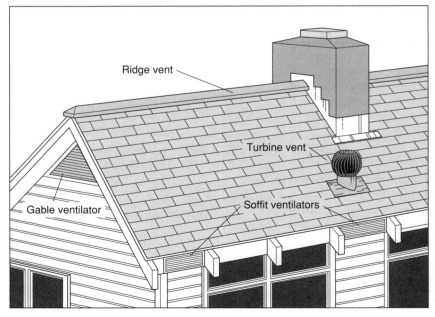

Controlling Ice & Snow on the Roof

Winter storms can wreak havoc on your roof. Ice dams that form at the eaves can create leaks, and snow can slide off the roof in mini-avalanches that bring roofing material and gutters down, too. You can prevent most problems by keeping your gutters clean and by installing one of the devices described below.

Ice Dams

Ice dams (see illustration below) can result from alternate thawing and freezing of the snow on the roof in a period of warm days and cold nights, or from heat loss through the roof of a poorly insulated and badly ventilated house. These frozen blockages at the eaves can cause the water from melting snow to back up under the shingles and leak into the house.

■ *De-icing tapes* (shown at upper right). These are electrically heated

COLD-CLIMATE HARDWARE

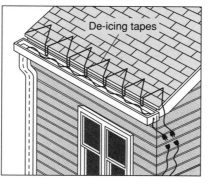

De-icing tapes

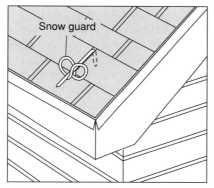

Snow guard

ICE DAM

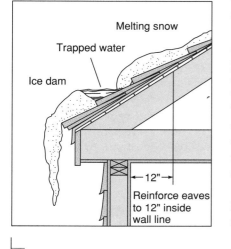

Melting snow
Trapped water
Ice dam
12"
Reinforce eaves to 12" inside wall line

cables, installed along the roof eaves and in the gutters and downspouts. They facilitate proper drainage of melting snow and ice so ice dams don't form.

Insulated for safety, the tapes are clipped to shingles in a zigzag pattern (or run along gutters and downspouts) and plugged into a weatherproof electrical outlet. Their heat creates miniature drainage channels for water that otherwise would back up behind ice dams or freeze inside downspouts.

Look for de-icing tapes at home-improvement centers or roofing supply companies. To in-

stall them, follow the manufacturer's instructions.

■ *Fans and soffit vents.* You can prevent ice dams that result from poor ventilation: install an attic fan and soffit vents (see the illustration on page 73, center) to vent warm attic air that might otherwise melt the snow on the roof. Soffit vents come in a variety of styles.

■ *Eaves reinforcement.* For extra protection on a section of roof where ice dams form, reinforce the eaves area by installing a sheet of roll roofing, roofing felt, or special membrane under the shingles to extend 12 inches inside the interior wall line. This is easiest to do when a new roof is being put on. (See pages 61 and 65 for more information.)

Each type of roofing requires a particular treatment; check your local building code to learn which is best for your situation.

Snow Buildup

Snow tends to slide off roofs like an avalanche, tearing gutters from their fastenings, ripping away roofing materials, and smashing plants or other objects on the ground below.

To help hold snow in place, you can attach metal snow guards in staggered rows over the roof. They come in several styles, including long, narrow ones for use over doorways. Check the manufacturer's directions on how many to use and how to install them.

INSULATION & BARRIERS

How well are your roof and walls insulated? If you're re-roofing or re-siding your home, remember that this gives you an opportunity to beef up your insulation relatively easily.

DOES YOUR HOME NEED MORE?

Resistance to heat flow is measured by an "R-value"—the higher, the greater. The total R-value of a roof or wall is the sum of the individual R-values of the roofing or siding materials, sheathing, and insulation.

Recommended minimum R-values of insulation for exterior walls are R-11 in mild climates and R-19 in severe climates. Recommended minimums for roofs or ceilings are R-19 for mild and R-38 for severe climates.

Different insulating materials have different R-values. For example, foam has an R-value of 5.3 or more per inch, whereas fiberglass blankets run about R-3.3 per inch. If your attic currently has some type of loose-fill material, figure R-2 to R-3 per inch when you're determining whether or not you need more. If walls or attic have blanket insulation, calculate the 3½-inch-thick blankets at R-11 and the 6-inch-thick blankets at R-19.

TYPES OF INSULATION

Houses are insulated using a variety of techniques and materials. The most common do-it-yourself materials are mineral-fiber (fiberglass or rock wool) batts and blankets. They're easy to install in an attic space or between exposed wall studs, as discussed here.

If you'll be removing the existing roof deck, you can insulate between ceiling joists at the same time—and avoid crawling through a cramped, dark attic. If you'll be peeling off siding and exposing the wall studs, you have a perfect opportunity to insulate the walls from the outside.

But if you can't insulate between ceiling joists—say, your house has exposed-beam ceilings—or if you'll be adding new siding over existing material, you must consider other options.

For exposed-beam ceilings or masonry basement walls, rigid-board insulation is often the best answer. Made from compressed, asphalt-impregnated fiberboard or from any of several types of expanded foam, rigid-board insulation panels may also be used as exterior sheathing under siding, as underlayment for roofs, around foundations, and on inner surfaces of interior walls. Panels come with a variety of facings. With foil facings, they reflect radiant heat and also serve as vapor barriers.

Look for materials specified as environmentally safe; some foams are being phased out because they employ ozone-damaging chlorofluoro-carbons (CFCs) as blowing agents.

Another option for attics or covered walls—as, for example, when you're re-siding over existing siding—is blown-in, loose-fill insulation. This comes in several forms: mineral wool, vermiculite, and, the most common, cellulose. For an attic, the blow-in method is fast. For covered walls, it is tedious, since a separate hole must be drilled in the siding to fill each stud cavity. Alternatively, you could have a contractor insulate the stud cavities with spray-in foam—an option that might be preferable because of the higher R-value of foam and because foam provides its own vapor barrier.

VAPOR BARRIERS

Taking a shower, cooking, washing dishes, even just breathing can put a

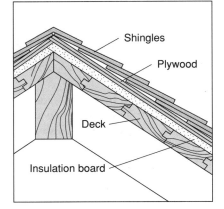

EXPOSED-BEAM CEILING

Shingles

Plywood

Deck

Insulation board

surprising amount of water into the air in a typical home—5 to 10 pounds a day. If you wash and dry clothes, you may be adding another 30 pounds.

Because heat always moves to a colder location, in winter this warm, moist interior air passes through walls, roofs, and floors. As the air moves, moisture condenses on the cold inner faces of the exterior surfaces. Eventually, it blisters outside paint, forms stains inside, and can rot the structure. And it saturates insulation, greatly reducing its effective R-value.

A moisture barrier repels the moist air before it gets through the insulation to the colder part of the wall.

Blanket insulation is available with attached foil vapor barriers. If you are insulating with loose fill or with blankets or batts that don't have an attached barrier, you can install a separate barrier of 2-mil (or thicker) polyethylene sheeting.

You must be very careful to put the vapor barrier on the warm-in-winter side of the insulation—in other words, toward the inside of the house. Before insulating a ceiling (the attic floor), you can staple strips of polyethylene between the joists or you can lay sheets of it over them, allowing the polyethylene to drape fully into each cavity. You can stretch a continuous sheet of polyethylene across the inside faces of wall studs and staple it in place. Be sure to keep the barrier, which is flammable, at least 3 inches away from any heat-producing equipment, such as recessed light fixtures or fans.

AIR INFILTRATION BARRIERS

A relatively new type of barrier, "house wrap" is a permeable film made of high-density polyethylene fibers. Sold in 8-foot-wide sheets, this material is stretched and stapled or nailed around the perimeter walls of the house, over the top of sheathing. Unlike a standard vapor barrier, which is applied to the inner face of a wall to keep moisture-laden air from being trapped in the stud cavity, this film is applied to the outside, allowing condensation to escape through the wall but eliminating most incoming drafts.

INSTALLING BLANKETS & BATTS

Tools for installing insulation include a sharp utility knife for cutting blankets or batts and a lightweight hand stapler for fastening them to studs or joists. To insulate dark areas in attics or under floors, you'll need at least one portable light with a 50-foot cord.

To protect your skin, eyes, nose, and lungs from irritation, be sure to wear gloves, plastic goggles, and a dust mask.

Insulating the attic. Unless your attic will be used as living space, you need insulate only between the joists of the ceilings of the rooms below the attic. These ceilings won't support you, so lay a few boards over the joists to serve as temporary flooring while you work.

If your insulation blankets or batts have an attached vapor barrier, lay them between the joists with the vapor barrier facing down. When you're working with a separate vapor barrier, fasten it first to the sides of the joists, then lay batts or blankets on top. Be sure the insulation extends over the top plates of walls below, but don't cover soffit vents or block air flow to them.

Peel the vapor barrier back at least 3 inches from heat producers, such as light fixtures and fans, and from chimneys, stovepipes, and flues. When possible, slip batts underneath electrical wiring.

If your attic is to be finished as living space, plan to insulate between rafters, collar beams, short "knee wall" studs, and gable studs instead of between joists. You can staple batts or blankets directly to the edges of rafters and studs, but be sure not to block any vent openings at the soffits. Staple the vapor barrier in place after insulation is installed.

Insulating walls. Normally, you install insulation from inside a room during construction, before wallboard is added. But if you're adding insulation when siding has been stripped from the house's exterior, you'll be working from the outside.

Precut 4-foot batts are simpler to handle if you're insulating a standard 8-foot wall with fire blocks at 4-foot heights, though blankets can be easily cut. It's best to choose insulation with an attached vapor barrier.

Cut batts or blankets to length with a straightedge and sharp utility knife, using the top plate, sole plate, or fire block to back your cuts. Size the pieces slightly long to ensure a tight fit.

Place the vapor barrier against the inside wall, staying clear of any heat-producing fixtures.

Stuff insulation scraps into cracks and small spaces between rough framing and the jambs of windows and doors. Also stuff the spaces behind electrical conduit, outlet and switch boxes, and other obstructions.

ATTIC INSULATION

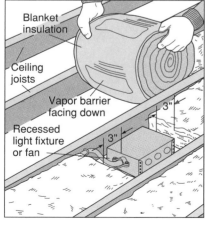

Blanket insulation

Ceiling joists

Vapor barrier facing down

3"

Recessed light fixture or fan

3"

ATTIC AIR FLOW

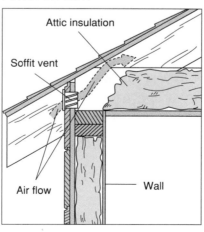

Attic insulation

Soffit vent

Air flow

Wall

WALL INSULATION

ROOFING
INSTALLATION

O nce you've prepared the roof deck, you're ready to begin applying the new roofing material. Depending on the product you've chosen and the type of roof your house has, this job can range from a fairly simple but tedious task to an exacting challenge. Be sure you're up for it: chances are, if you decide to bring in a professional roofer halfway through the project, you'll end up paying more than you would have spent for a complete job. Few contractors like to finish a roofing job that someone else has started—and even fewer will guarantee the work.

As discussed on page 52, some roofing materials lend themselves to do-it-yourself installation and some do not. Asphalt shingles are considered to be quite easy to apply. Other materials commonly installed by homeowners include roll roofing, wood shingles, and wood shakes. Among the many other roofing materials available—ceramic and concrete tile, metal shingles, sheet metal, and more—ease of installation varies widely. Skilled novices can handle some; other types should be left to professional roofers.

With this in mind, this chapter offers complete, step-by-step guidance for installing asphalt shingles, roll roofing, and wood shingles and shakes. In addition, as a general reference for experienced home improvers, it outlines basic techniques for installing certain types of masonry and metal roofing. This book does not discuss how to install slate, sheet-metal roofing, built-up, single-ply, polyurethane, or other materials meant to be installed solely by professionals.

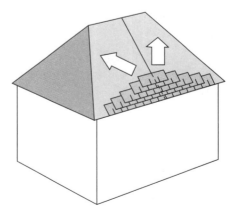

BASIC ROOFING TIPS

Before you begin your installation job, familiarize yourself with the following general roofing procedures and review the safety tips on page 51.

Manufacturers' directions may differ slightly from those given here. Veering from the specifications can void your warranty. Carefully follow any instructions that come with the roofing materials you buy.

FROM THE BOTTOM UP

Nearly all roofing materials are installed by beginning at the eaves and working toward the ridge (though one type of professionally installed interlocking metal roofing shingle is applied from the ridge down). With nearly all shingles except masonry and metal, the first course is doubled to provide the proper thickness and lapped coverage necessary for complete protection.

If you're roofing over an old roof, especially if covering old asphalt shingles with new ones, new shingles may conveniently line up with the butts of the old ones. But on many old roofs and all new decks, you must snap chalk lines to keep shingles (or tiles) properly aligned. Battens are necessary for some materials, as discussed on page 63. Their placement is critical to shingle alignment.

Whether you're snapping chalk lines, installing battens, or simply placing shingles on old roofing, you must realize that most roofs are not square and that shingle courses seldom meet evenly at the ridge. Likewise, shingles usually don't end in even increments at the rakes. Before you lay materials, measure your roof to gauge how shingles will fall. As you work, recheck measurements occasionally, and compensate gradually for discrepancies—either by shortening the exposure on courses near the ridge or by trimming materials at the least obvious rake.

To expedite your work, once the first courses are down, don't shingle a single course all the way across the roof. Stay at one point and lay a fan-shaped spread of five or so courses. Then move sideways and start another fan. (Working this way with asphalt shingles also hides any color variations from bundle to bundle.)

Whether you should begin at the right or left corner or in the center of the roof depends on the type of roof you have, on the materials you're using, and on whether you're more comfortable moving from right to left or left to right.

Gabled roofs. If you have a gabled roof and are right-handed, begin at the left rake so you can swing your right arm in an arc as you work. If you're left-handed, start on the right.

If you're putting down interlocking masonry or metal shingles or tiles, the product design may dictate which rake you must use as the starting point in order for components to hook together properly (see page 82).

Hipped roofs. Since hipped roofs have no rake, you start from the center when installing most materials. Locate the center by snapping a vertical chalk line equidistant from the corners; then work outward from this line in both directions.

PROPER FASTENING

Proper fastening is an essential part of good roofing. It depends on three things: selecting the right type and length of nail or fastener, using the proper number of fasteners, and putting fasteners in the right places. In this chapter, type, size, number, and placement of fasteners is discussed with each kind of roofing.

Though the classic way to attach shingles is with a hammer and nails, many roofers prefer to use a pneumatic stapler or nailer for asphalt shingles, since it makes the work go so much faster. You can rent one to speed your own job. But don't use it on particularly hot or cold days—on a hot day, a fastener could go right through an asphalt shingle, and on a cold day, it could break the material.

ROOFING SEQUENCE

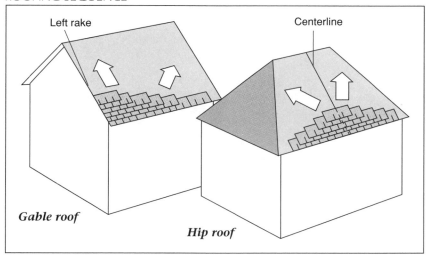

Left rake

Centerline

Gable roof

Hip roof

APPLYING ASPHALT SHINGLES

Standard three-tab asphalt shingles are one of the easiest of all roofing materials to install. They are a manageable weight to carry and a breeze to cut and nail. In addition, the 12- by 36-inch shingles, when given a standard weather exposure of 5 inches, cover large areas quickly.

Before installation, review instructions on valley flashings (see page 65).

Cutting. To cut an asphalt shingle, turn it face down on a flat surface. Hold a carpenter's square or straightedge across the line you want to cut and, using a sharp utility knife, score the back of the shingle. Then just bend the shingle to break it across the scored line. (For short or irregular cuts, you don't need a guide.)

Fastening. For asphalt shingles, use 12-gauge galvanized roofing nails

with ⅜-inch-diameter heads. Proper nail length depends on the nature of the material you're nailing the shingles to: use 1¼-inch-long nails for new roofs, 1½-inch nails for roofing over an asphalt roof, and 1¾-inch nails for roofing over a wood roof (though, as discussed on page 62, this practice is often discouraged).

For comments on using a pneumatic nailer or stapler, see page 75.

STARTER COURSE

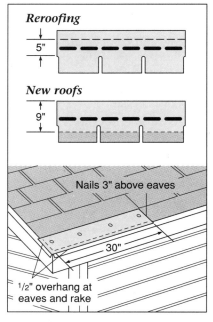

Reroofing

5"

New roofs

9"

Nails 3" above eaves

30"

½" overhang at eaves and rake

FIRST COURSE

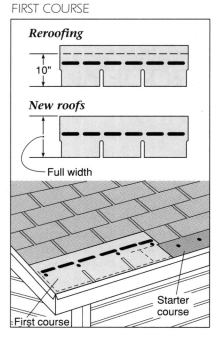

Reroofing

10"

New roofs

Full width

First course

Starter course

Starter course and first course. A narrow starter row of shingles runs the length of the eaves to form a base for the first full course of shingles. Before laying the starter course, first measure the width of the roof along the eaves so you can prepare enough shingles to cover the distance.

When you're reroofing over asphalt shingles, make the starter course 5 inches wide to match the ex-

NAILING ASPHALT SHINGLES

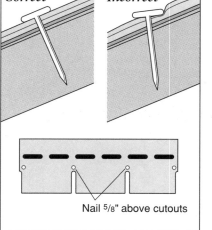

Correct   *Incorrect*

Nail ⅝" above cutouts

CHALK LINES FOR ASPHALT SHINGLES

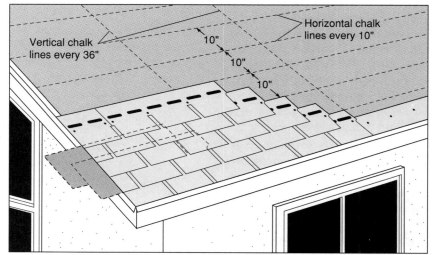

Vertical chalk lines every 36"

Horizontal chalk lines every 10"

10"

10"

10"

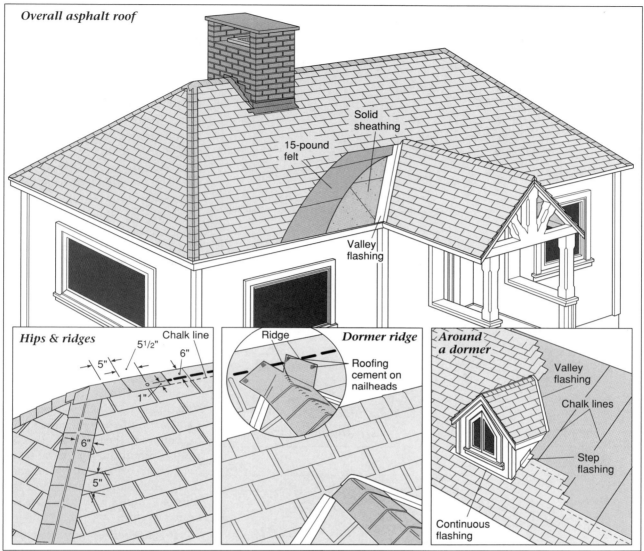

Overall asphalt roof

Solid sheathing

15-pound felt

Valley flashing

Hips & ridges

5½"

5"

6"

Chalk line

1"

6"

5"

Ridge

Dormer ridge

Roofing cement on nailheads

Around a dormer

Valley flashing

Chalk lines

Step flashing

Continuous flashing

posure of the existing first course (see the drawing on the facing page, top left). Cut 5 inches off tabs and 2 inches from top edges of 12-inch-wide shingles. For a new roof, use a 9-inch-wide starter course; cut 3 inches off tabs of 12-inch-wide shingles (or use a 9-inch-wide strip of asphalt roll roofing).

Starting at one rake, apply the starter course along the eaves with the shingles' weather side down. Trim 6 inches off the first shingle's length to offset the cutouts in the starter and first courses.

Allowing a ½-inch overhang at both eaves and rakes and $\frac{1}{16}$ inch as spacing between shingles, fasten the shingles to the deck, using four nails each, nailed 3 inches above the eaves. Position these nails 1 and 12 inches in from each end.

To lay the first course over the starter course on a new roof, use full-width shingles. When reroofing, use a 10-inch-wide course to cover the two 5-inch exposures of the existing first two courses. Cut 2 inches from the top edges of as many shingles as were needed for the starter course.

Allow the same ½-inch overhang at the rakes and eaves and $\frac{1}{16}$ inch be-tween shingles. Nail the first course over the starter course, using four nails per shingle. Space nails 5⅝ inch-es above the butt line and 12 inches in from each end (or according to manufacturer's instructions).

Successive courses. When you lay the second and successive courses, your main concern is proper align-ment of the shingles—both horizon-tally and vertically. Aligning shingles horizontally for a new roof or on felt

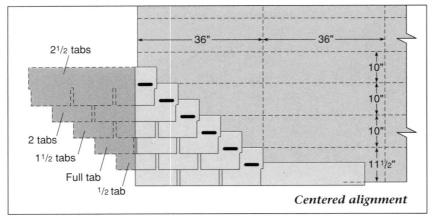

2¹/₂ tabs

2 tabs

1¹/₂ tabs

Full tab

¹/₂ tab

36" 36"

10"

10"

10"

11¹/₂"

Centered alignment

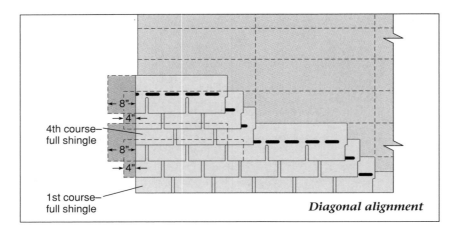

4th course—
full shingle

8"
4"
8"
4"

1st course—
full shingle

Diagonal alignment

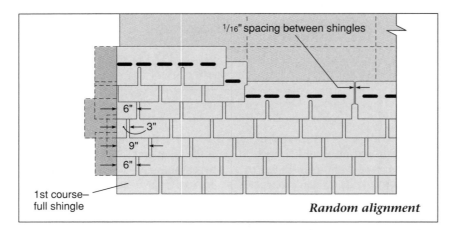

¹/₁₆" spacing between shingles

6"
3"
9"
6"

1st course—
full shingle

Random alignment

of every shingle along the first course. Continue to the top of the roof.

If you're working with standard three-tab shingles, you can produce centered, diagonal, or random roof patterns by adjusting the length of the shingle that begins each course, as shown in the drawing at left.

Centered alignment creates the most uniform roof appearance, but is also the most difficult pattern to achieve: cutouts on shingle edges must line up within ¼ inch of the two courses above and below.

Diagonal alignment is a little more forgiving of slight errors in calculation, since the joints of four courses in a row are offset.

Random alignment produces a more rustic appearance and is the easiest of the three patterns to lay: you just offset the joints of three courses in a row by at least 3 inches.

Hips and ridges. If you haven't purchased ready-made hip and ridge shingles, cut 12-inch squares from standard shingles. Bend each square to conform to the roof ridge. (In cold weather, warm shingles before bending.) Then, before you begin, snap chalk lines along each side of the ridge and along each hip, 6 inches from the center.

If your roof has hips, start with them. Beginning with a double layer of shingles at the bottom of one hip, work toward the ridge, applying shingles with a 5-inch exposure. The edge of each shingle should line up with your chalk mark. Use two nails, one on each side, 5½ inches from the butt and 1 inch from the outside edge. Repeat for each hip.

To shingle the ridge, start at the end opposite the direction from which the wind most often blows. Using nails long enough to penetrate the ridge board securely (about 2 inches long), apply the shingles in the manner just described. Dab the exposed nailheads of the last shingle with plastic roofing cement.

over an old roof is simply a matter of snapping chalk lines; if you're reroofing without adding felt, just place the new shingles against the butts of old ones. If you're using chalk lines as guides, snap them every 10 inches from the bottom of the first course.

Then, as you move toward the ridge, the upper edge of every other course of shingles should line up against a chalk line.

Before you start the second row of shingles, also snap vertical chalk lines from the roof ridge to one end

INSTALLING ROLL ROOFING

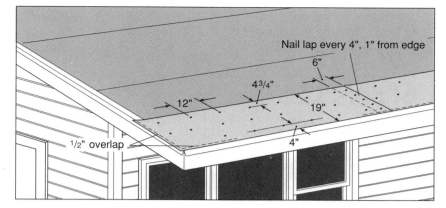

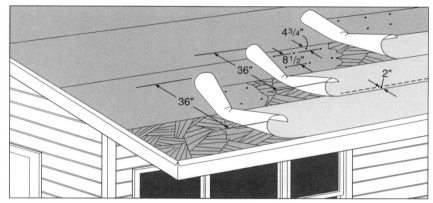

Roll roofing is often chosen for outbuildings because it's economical and relatively easy to use. Rolls of 36-inch-wide asphalt roofing are unfurled horizontally across the roof and applied directly over solid sheathing, with the 17-inch-wide strip of mineral surface exposed and the 19-inch-wide selvage (uncoated) portion lapped underneath the next strip up the roof. Each layer is bonded to the next with plastic roofing cement.

Starter course and first course. Roll roofing is easy to cut with a sharp utility knife. Run a 19-inch-wide strip from rake to rake. If one piece isn't long enough, overlap adjoining lengths by 6 inches. Fasten one end to the roof with nails spaced every 4 inches (and set in 1 inch from the edge); lap and cement the second piece to the first.

Lay the starter strip along the eaves with a ½-inch overlap at the eaves and rakes, and fasten it to the deck with three rows of nails spaced 12 inches apart. Position the nails 4¾ inches from the upper edge, 4 inches above the bottom edge, and along the middle between these two rows, staggering the nails as shown above.

For new roofs, use 12-gauge galvanized nails with ⅜-inch-diameter heads and 1-inch shanks. For reroofing, longer nails may be necessary to penetrate old materials and reach ¾ inch into a wood deck or completely through a plywood deck.

Next, spread plastic roofing cement of a brushable consistency over the starter sheet.

Then overlay a 36-inch-wide sheet and nail along the top (uncoat-ed) 19-inch portion; place the nails in two rows, the first 4¾ inches below the upper edge and the second 8½ inches below the first row.

Successive courses. Using roofing cement, bond each layer of roll roofing to the previous one in the manner just described, lapping the mineral-covered portion over the uncoated selvage of the course below. Continue toward the ridge.

Hips and ridges. Cut enough 12- by 36-inch rectangles from rolls to cover hips and ridges. Also cut enough 12- by 17-inch rectangles to double the starter shingles at each hip and ridge. Then snap a chalk line along both sides of each hip or ridge, 5½ inches from the center.

Bend pieces lengthwise and, starting at the bottom of the hips or the end of the ridge opposite the prevailing wind, fasten as shown. Fix the upper 19 inches of each shingle to the roof with nails placed every 4 inches, 1 inch from the outside edge. Cement the lower, 17-inch portion in place.

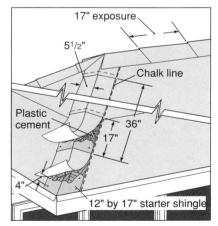

APPLYING WOOD SHINGLES & SHAKES

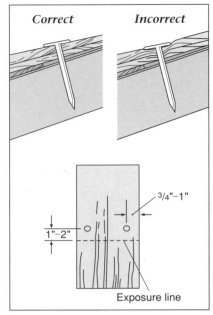

Exposure line

Though wood shingles and shakes appear similar, application techniques are quite different. Shingles are best applied to open sheathing (see page 58) without underlayment, a method that allows plenty of air circulation around the undersides. Because the rougher texture of shakes allows a certain amount of air flow, they may be applied over either open or solid sheathing. But with the more irregular shakes, underlayment is installed between each course, a lapped construction that provides a good weather barrier.

When applying wood shingles or shakes, always position the tapered end at the upper side of the roof, with the thicker end down. If the wood has a sawn side and a rough side, face the rough side to the weather.

Correct exposure for wood shingles and shakes depends on their length and on the slope of your roof. Here are some recommendations:

MAXIMUM EXPOSURE SHINGLES & SHAKES

	3-in-12 to 4-in-12 slopes	4-in-12 and steeper slopes
Shingles		
For #1 (blue label shingles)		
16"	3¾"	5"
18"	4¼"	5½"
24"	5¾"	7½"
Shakes		
18"	—	7½"
24"	—	10"

Cutting. To make straight cuts in shingles, simply slice through them with a roofer's hatchet. Heavier wood shakes can either be sawn or split along the grain with the hatchet.

When it's necessary to make an angled cut for a valley, lay the shingle in place and use a straightedge to mark the angle of the cut. Then score the shingle with a utility knife and break it against a hard edge. Wood shakes must be sawn.

Fastening. Use two rustproof nails per shingle or shake. Nails for wood shingles should be 14½-gauge with ⁷⁄₃₂-inch-diameter heads. Use 1¼-inch-long nails for a new roof of 16- or 18-inch shingles; use 1½-inch nails for a new roof of 24-inch shingles. Longer nails may be needed to penetrate old roof surfaces and reach ¾ inch into or through the deck. Above visible roof overhangs, use shorter nails.

For wood shakes, the preferred choice is 13-gauge nails with ⁷⁄₃₂-inch-diameter heads. Use 2-inch-long nails unless longer ones are required.

When fastening shingles, place the nails ¾ to 1 inch in from each side and 1 to 2 inches above the butt line for the next course. Nails for shakes should be positioned 1 inch in from the sides. Don't dimple nails into wood with the final blow.

Starter course and first course. Combine the starter and first courses by laying the shingles or shakes one on top of another (see drawings on the facing page, top). Overhang this double course 1½ inches at the eaves and rakes.

See "Getting Started" (page 48), for information on applying flash-

APPLYING WOOD SHINGLES

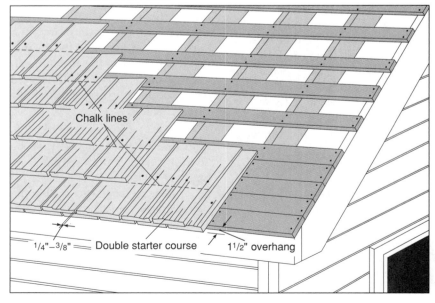

Chalk lines

¼"–³⁄₈"   Double starter course   1½" overhang

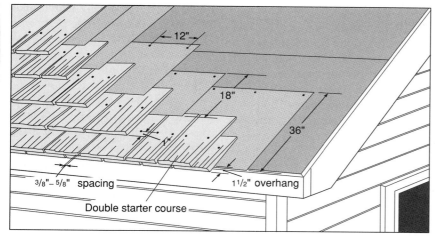

APPLYING WOOD SHAKES

12"

18"

36"

1"

3/8"– 5/8" spacing

1 1/2" overhang

Double starter course

ings, underlayment, and protective membranes along the eaves. Nail the starter-course shingles or shakes in place, overhanging eaves and rakes by 1½ inches. Use short, 15-inch shakes as the starter course; these can be ready-made or cut from standard shakes. Allow spacing of ¼ to ⅜ inch between shingles and ⅜ to ⅝ inch between shakes so the wood can expand and contract.

The first course goes directly on top of the starter course; be sure to offset joints between the shingles of each layer by 1½ inches.

Successive courses. As you lay each of the next courses, offset joints by at least 1½ inches so that no joints in any three successive courses align.

To line up wood shingles horizontally, snap a chalk line at the proper exposure over the doubled starter/first course, or use the gauge on a roofer's hatchet as an exposure guide. Then lay the butts of shingles in the next course at the chalk line. Nail the course down and repeat the procedure until you reach the ridge.

When aligning wood shakes, install "shake liner" roofing felt interlays between courses as you work toward the ridge. Measure a distance twice the planned exposure from the butt of the starter/first course, place the bottom edge of an 18-inch-wide

strip of 15-pound (minimum) felt at that line, and nail every 12 inches along the top edge of the felt. Overlap vertical joints of the felt by 4 inches.

Then snap a chalk line on the starter/first course for the proper exposure (or use your roofer's hatchet as a guide). Nail the second course, place the next felt strip, and continue this way until you reach the ridge.

At the hips or the ridge, let the last courses of shingles or shakes hang over; snap a chalk line above the center of the ridge board and trim off all the ends at once. Cover the hip or ridge with a strip of roofing felt at least 8 inches wide.

Hips and ridges. Using factory-made hip and ridge shingles, double the starter courses at the bottom of each hip and at the end of the ridge, as shown in the drawing below right.

Exposure should equal the weather exposure of the wood shingles or shakes on the roof planes. Start the ridge shingles at the end of the ridge opposite the prevailing wind. Use nails long enough to penetrate the layers of material and extend into the ridge board (usually 2 or 2½ inches). Use two nails per side of each shingle, locating them where the overlapping shingle will cover them by 1 to 2 inches. Dab plastic roofing cement on the last two nailheads.

ALIGNING SHINGLES

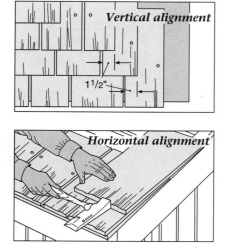

Vertical alignment

1 1/2"

Horizontal alignment

ALIGNING SHAKES

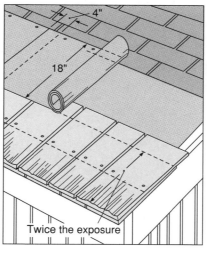

4"

18"

Twice the exposure

HIPS & RIDGES

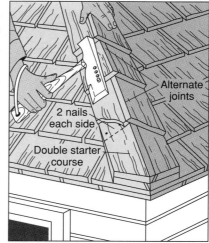

Alternate joints

2 nails each side

Double starter course

INSTALLING TILE ROOFS

Unless you have plenty of energy and are particularly handy, you're better off leaving installation of masonry tile roofing to a professional. The tiles are heavy to handle, and all cuts must be made with a masonry blade on a power saw. In addition, most masonry tile is unforgiving of small errors in layout.

Between barrel-shaped and flat tiles, flat ones are much easier to apply. (Curved Spanish-style tiles require special flashing and sealing techniques and are prone to break when you walk on them. Their installation should be left to professionals.)

If you decide to install flat tiles, be sure to request complete specifications from the supplier. Many kinds of masonry tile are made, as discussed on page 16, and each type has its own installation requirements. The pointers offered here are meant only as a general guide.

Special preparation notes. If you're not sure the roof's structure can handle the tiles' heavy weight, check with your building department or a structural engineer.

Most masonry-tile roofs require solid sheathing and 30-pound or heavier underlayment. Some professional roofers recommend putting one vent flashing on the felt, over each vent stack and then working a second flashing into the tiles as you lay them.

Some tiles require battens, and hips and ridges usually require nailers—a 2 by 3 set on edge along each hip and a 2 by 2 placed along the peak of each ridge to support curved or angled hip and ridge tiles. As shown in the drawing below, hold the hip nailers back from the eaves about 6 inches to hide them from view. If needed, nail a 1 by 3 flat against the rafters along the rakes to support rake tiles. Since you don't double-cover along the eaves (as with shingling), you need to nail a redwood, cedar, or pressure-treated 1-by-2 strip or special eaves metal along the eaves to give starter tiles the proper pitch.

When laying out battens or chalk lines, you want to avoid ending up with an odd-shaped course of tiles at the top. To accomplish this, measure the distance from eaves to ridge, then calculate the necessary incre-

MASONRY TILE ROOF

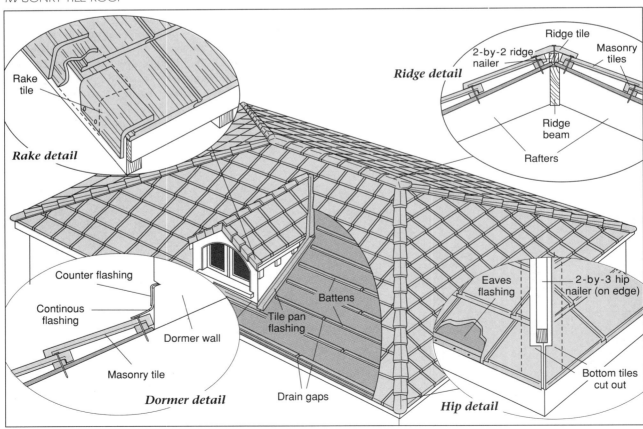

Rake tile

Rake detail

Ridge detail

2-by-2 ridge nailer

Ridge tile

Masonry tiles

Ridge beam

Rafters

Counter flashing

Continous flashing

Dormer wall

Masonry tile

Dormer detail

Battens

Tile pan flashing

Drain gaps

Eaves flashing

2-by-3 hip nailer (on edge)

Bottom tiles cut out

Hip detail

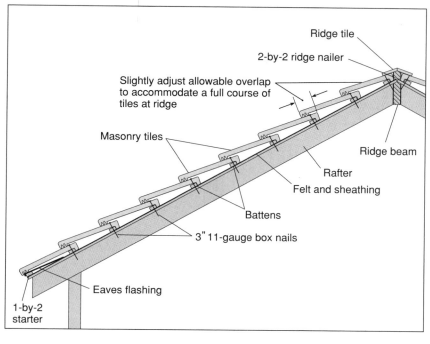

Ridge tile

2-by-2 ridge nailer

Slightly adjust allowable overlap to accommodate a full course of tiles at ridge

Masonry tiles

Ridge beam

Rafter

Felt and sheathing

Battens

3" 11-gauge box nails

Eaves flashing

1-by-2 starter

Successive courses. Continue up the roof. When you've accumulated a few tiles that need to be cut for hips or valleys, stop fastening field tiles and cut all the custom tiles you need at one time. Use plastic roofing cement to secure particularly small pieces or any that have had their nailing areas trimmed off.

Hips, ridges, and rakes. Most masonry tile systems include special tiles for hips, ridges, and rakes (rake tiles are sometimes called "barge" tiles). When you've placed all field tiles, begin with the rake and ridge tiles, as shown on the facing page.

Working from the eaves toward the ridge, cut the hip tiles at the lower ends of hips to conceal the hip nailers and lap the tiles to provide the proper exposure. Embed the undersides of the butt ends of rake and ridge tiles in dabs of plastic roofing cement before nailing them on. Repeat for each hip.

At the ridge, work from the ends toward the center, using the same methods as for hips. Dab the exposed nailheads of the last tile with plastic roofing cement. Apply rake tiles the same way, working from eaves to gable.

ments within the maximum allowable shingle exposure (manufacturers' specifications give you this maximum); adjust the positions of battens or chalk lines accordingly. Be sure to nail battens to rafters, not just to sheathing.

When walking on masonry tile, take care not to crack it. Place your feet parallel to the eaves on the lower few inches of the tile, avoiding stepping on overlapping edges or corners.

Cutting. To cut or trim tiles for valleys, hips, rakes, ridges, and obstructions, use a circular saw with an abrasive or diamond-tipped blade. Wear safety glasses and a dust mask when you work.

Mark each tile with a guideline so you'll know where to cut the pieces to fit valleys and vent pipes. Then make straight cuts from the tile's edge toward the center, following the guideline. If necessary, break the tile between two cuts, using a brick set or cold chisel. Or, for a longer crosscut, you can make a "dip cut," slowly lowering the power saw's blade into the center of the tile.

Dust created by cutting is slippery and can stain the roof if left on overnight, so sweep or blow off the roof with a leaf blower periodically.

Fastening. Many flat tiles have lugs on the undersides to hook over battens. They have pre-punched nail holes. Tile nails are usually 11-gauge corrosion-resistant box nails 3 inches long or long enough to penetrate through a solid deck. Use shorter nails at exposed eaves.

First course. With most types, you start flush with the right rake and work your way toward the left, letting the ends of the first course protrude over the fascia about 1 inch. Overlap their edges and nail in place, being careful not to crack tiles with the hammer. Stop short of the roof's hips.

With some masonry tiles, joints between tiles are meant to be staggered up the roof, like those of wood shingles and shakes. But some types are meant to have edge joints aligned with all other courses. Be sure you know which method is intended for your material.

TYPICAL MASONRY TILES

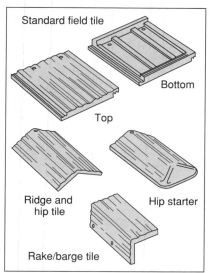

Standard field tile

Bottom

Top

Ridge and hip tile

Hip starter

Rake/barge tile

INSTALLING METAL SHINGLES

O f the many different kinds of metal roofing products available (see page 20), only a few can be installed by homeowners. Because most sheet-metal systems and interlocking metal-shingle panels require specialized knowledge, skills, and tools, they are sold only through certified installers.

There are, however, a few types of metal shingles that experienced home-improvers can manage. Most of these are formed, individual shingles of aluminum, copper, or coated steel that are designed to interlock. They are extremely lightweight, making them easy to carry, and some can be used on roofs with as little pitch as as 2 in 12. If you decide to install your own metal shingles, be sure to request complete manufacturer's specifications and installation instruc-

tions; techniques vary widely from one product to another.

Most manufacturers make color-matched flashings. Some metal-shingle systems include starter strips, continuous valleys, hip and ridge caps, end-wall (continuous) flashing, side-wall (dormer) flashing, gable-end flashing, vent flashing, and touch-up paint. Even so, special situations often call for flashings or pieces that require custom fabrication. Some makers sell matching roll or sheet stock that a local sheet-metal shop can form to your needs.

Most metal shingles are meant to be applied over solid sheathing. Some types require an underlayment of 15- or 30-pound felt; others call for an interleaf of 18-inch-wide, 15-pound shake liner between courses.

Cutting and folding. The only metal shingles you should attempt to install are those you can cut with tin snips (heavier materials entail far too much work). You may also need to buy or rent a folding tool and, for some types of shingle, a hand seamer. With most materials, you can make a straight fold simply by clamping the

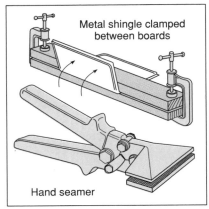

Metal shingle clamped between boards

Hand seamer

shingle between two 2 by 4s and bending it.

Fastening. To prevent electrolysis (a corrosive action that occurs when two dissimilar metals contact each other), use fasteners and flashings made from the same type of metal as the shingles: aluminum nails for aluminum shingles, bronze nails for copper shingles, galvanized steel nails for steel shingles. Fasten through pre-punched nail holes or nailing flanges.

First course. Follow the manufacturer's directions for application of shingles along the first course. A standard way is to begin at the lower left corner, fitting the first shingle into a special gable-end flashing that runs along the rake. Nail the first shingle in place and continue along the eaves, interlocking shingles and nailing them as specified.

Successive courses. With some types, the second course begins with a half-shingle, in order to offset joints. All shingles are interlocked and nailed, like the first course.

Hips and ridges. At hips and ridges, you generally cut and bend the shingles over the top. Then you add special hip and ridge shingles—on hips working from the bottom to the top and on ridges starting at the end facing the prevailing wind.

METAL-SHINGLE ROOF

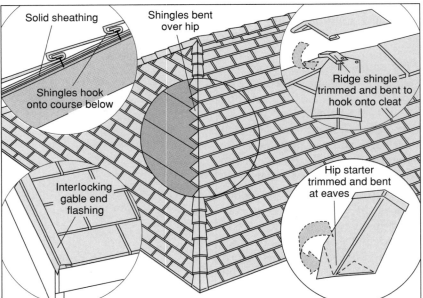

Solid sheathing

Shingles bent over hip

Shingles hook onto course below

Ridge shingle trimmed and bent to hook onto cleat

Interlocking gable end flashing

Hip starter trimmed and bent at eaves

Exterior Caulking

Caulking compound fills gaps in exterior siding and roofing; seals out drafts, moisture, and insects; and seals in heated or cooled air. Several types are available. The best choice for an individual job depends on the particular materials, weather conditions, and budget. Compounds are rated by their expected life. As a rule, the more you spend, the longer the caulk will last. Though some products are rated to hold up for 30 or more years, all caulk eventually dries out and requires renewal—so check for cracked, loose, or missing caulk during maintenance inspections.

■ *Types of caulk.* The five basic types of exterior caulk are elastomers, butyl rubber, acrylic latex, non-acrylic latex, and oil-base. When making your choice, read labels carefully and consider the nature of the materials to which the caulk must adhere.

You can buy caulk in a disposable cartridge to be used with a half-barrel caulking gun; in a can for application with a full-barrel caulking gun or a putty knife; in a small squeeze tube; as "rope"; or in an aerosol-type can that squirts expanding foam into large gaps. The half-barrel gun with cartridge is the most popular dispenser, since it most easily produces an even bead of compound. Use rope caulk as temporary filler for very wide cracks or joints—it may not adhere for very long.

CAUTION: Before you buy any caulking material, read the labels. Some types won't work in cracks or joints less than ¼ inch wide; others work well only in narrow cracks. Note any precautions recommended and follow directions.

■ *Where to caulk.* Generally, caulk in areas where different surfaces meet. Here are some such places:

■ On the roof where two flashings meet; between a flashing and a roof or dormer surface; and to seal flashings where a chimney, flue, plumbing, electrical pipe, or skylight penetrates the roof surface.

■ On siding where the siding and trim meet at corners; around window and door frames; between poorly fitting pieces of siding; where pipes, framing members (such as exposed beams), and other protrusions pass through siding; and where the siding meets a foundation, patio, deck, or other distinct part of the house.

It's also wise to examine all of your interior window and door frames, especially between sliding door or window tracks and the sill or jamb.

■ *How to caulk.* First, remove old or damaged caulk. Dig it out or chip it off with a putty knife, screwdriver, or scraper. Then use a wire brush to remove debris and wipe the surface with a cloth soaked with solvent. Check the label to see if you need to prime the surface. Caulk on a dry day when the temperature is between 50° and 70°F.

Directions for using a half-barrel caulking gun appear at left. It may take practice to get an even bead of caulking compound. Hold the gun at a 45° angle to the surface; then, while moving the gun across the surface, squeeze the trigger consistently. Make sure the compound evenly fills the space between adjoining surfaces. If the crack is deep, apply two beads.

When using rope caulk, unroll the amount you need and use your fingers to stuff it into the crack.

HOW TO USE A CAULKING GUN

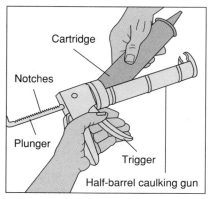

1) To load the gun, pull the plunger out (notches facing up). Insert the cartridge, bottom end first. Push the plunger in and rotate it so that the notches face down. Then pull the trigger.

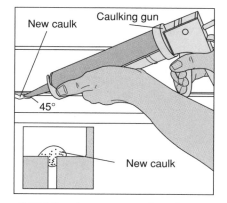

2) Holding the gun at a 45° angle to the joint, steadily squeeze the trigger as you move the gun carefully along the joint. Make sure the bead overlaps both sides of the crack evenly (see inset).

GUTTER SYSTEMS

R oofs shed water, but gutters and downspouts carry the water away. When reroofing or repairing the roof, inspect and repair gutters to be sure they're doing their job. If your gutters are in bad shape—or nonexistent—consider installing new ones.

Most gutters and downspouts are made of galvanized steel, aluminum, or vinyl, though you may find some made from wood or copper. Metal and wood types can be painted. Though professionally installed gutters are often extruded on site in order to be made seamless, systems you can assemble and install yourself are made of preformed parts—U-shaped troughs, elbows, downspouts, connectors, and so forth.

Gutters are attached to the eaves of the house with strap, bracket, or spike-and-ferrule hangers (see drawing below). Strap hangers are nailed onto the roof underneath roofing materials. With asphalt-shingle roofs, they can sometimes be installed after roofing; but for other materials, they must be installed before starter and first courses. Bracket hangers and spike-and-ferrule hangers mount on the fascia boards. Downspouts are attached by straps to exterior walls.

To work effectively, gutters and downspouts must be in good condition, must be sloped properly, and must be kept free of debris.

Maintaining gutter systems. Regular maintenance is crucial. In fall and spring, clean out debris. Then check the slope of the gutters by running water through them. If drainage is slow, reposition gutters: they should be tight against fascias and drop toward downspouts at a rate of 1 inch for every 20 linear feet. To correct low spots, adjust the hangers.

Test for weaknesses in gutters, downspouts, and fascia boards by probing with a thin screwdriver or knife. Also look for flaking or peeling paint, rust spots, broken hangers, and any holes or leaky joints.

Repairing fascias, gutters, and downspouts. If you find dry-rotted fascia boards, carve out the bad spots and fill with wood putty or replace the damaged section with a piece of well-seasoned lumber (applying a wood preservative first). Finish to match existing boards.

Tighten any loose hangers and replace any that are broken. Check that downspout straps are secured to the walls and that all elbow connections fit tightly.

Patch any leaky joints or holes in gutters (see the illustration on page 87), cleaning them thoroughly first. Seal pinholes with a dab of roofing cement. If a section of your gutter system is badly damaged, replace it.

Repaint the inside of wood gutters as necessary. Sand rust and corrosion on metal gutters and apply asphalt aluminum paint to the inside, rust-preventative zinc-base primer outside. Paint the outside of wood or metal gutters to match the house.

REPLACING GUTTER SYSTEMS

Gutters come in 4-, 5-, and 6-inch diameters; downspouts are available in 3- and 4-inch diameters. The size you use depends on the square footage of each roof's sections, as shown here:

Roof area (sq. ft.)	Gutter diameter	Downspout diameter
100–800	4"	3"
800–1,000	5"	3"
1,000–1,400	5"	4"
1,400+	6"	4"

Most manufacturers sell gutters in 10-foot lengths. Estimate the number of lengths you'll need based on the length of the eaves. Also count the number of fasteners and other fittings you'll need—including one connector for each length, caps for each end, inside and outside corners for each turn, one drop outlet and three straps for each downspout, and one hanger for every 3 feet of gutter. If your roof has overhangs, you'll also need elbows to connect each downspout to its drop outlet. For vinyl gutters, you may also need polyvinyl chloride (PVC) cement.

INSTALLING A SYSTEM

If you have a helper, assemble gutter runs on the ground, then fasten them along chalk lines to the fascia boards or to the lower edge of roof decking.

ANATOMY OF A GUTTER SYSTEM

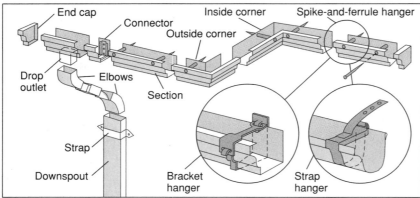

End cap
Connector
Inside corner
Spike-and-ferrule hanger
Outside corner
Drop outlet
Elbows
Section
Strap
Downspout
Bracket hanger
Strap hanger

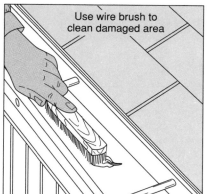
Use wire brush to clean damaged area

Apply roofing cement to 6" area on either side of damage

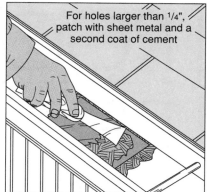
For holes larger than 1/4", patch with sheet metal and a second coat of cement

Snapping a chalk line. To provide the proper slope for a gutter system, position a chalk line immediately below where the gutter will be located, and tie it to nails at each end. Use a line level in order to be certain that the string is level, then lower the string at the downspout end to achieve a drop of 1 inch per 20 linear feet. Snap the chalk line and install the gutter against it.

Assembling the parts. Metal gutter parts either snap together or join with connectors. Caulk along both the inside of the connector and the undersides of the gutter sections, then push the ends together. Crimp the end of the connector over the edge of the gutter with pliers. Caulk joints and end caps.

Some vinyl systems use glue, but don't glue the downspouts into place. You may want to remove them completely when you're cleaning out debris.

Cutting gutters. Use a 2 by 4 as a support and a hacksaw (or, for vinyl, a fine-toothed handsaw) to cut gutter pieces. File down rough edges.

Fastening gutters to the roof. If you're working alone, tie a wire around one end of the gutter and hook it over a nail driven temporarily into the eaves. Nail the first hangers at the downspout end to position the outlet section accurately over a splash block. Work outward from that point. Use two hangers at each corner for support.

Connecting downspouts. Downspout parts fit one inside another and, on a house with overhangs, may be joined to the gutter assembly with elbows. On metal downspouts, drill two holes for metal screws to secure the downspout or elbow at the drop outlet.

To secure downspouts to wood siding, nail or screw straps in place; with stucco walls, use a masonry bit to drill holes for expansion bolts; with brick walls, drill holes with a masonry bit and drive in anchors for the screws. Coat the back of each strap with caulking compound or roofing cement to produce a seal.

IMPROVING DRAINAGE

Water flowing from your downspouts directly into the ground ends up alongside your house, causing the structure to settle.

To divert water, place a ready-made concrete or plastic splash block below an elbow attached to the downspout. Tilt the block so the water flows away from the house.

An alternative is a plastic or fabric sleeve that you attach directly to the downspout. Some sleeves are perforated to disperse the water over a large area; others unroll as the water flows through them, diverting drainage away from the house (the sleeve rolls back up once the water has drained).

INSTALLING A GUTTER SYSTEM

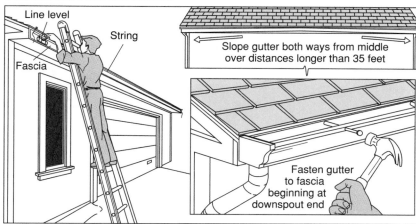
Line level
String
Fascia
Slope gutter both ways from middle over distances longer than 35 feet
Fasten gutter to fascia beginning at downspout end

ROOFING REPAIRS & MAINTENANCE

Installing a new roof is a job most people prefer to put off. As home improvements go, a new roof isn't nearly as satisfyingly visible as a fresh coat of paint or a remodeled bathroom—unless, of course, the existing roof has become an eyesore or no longer provides shelter from the elements. It makes sense to maintain your roof properly so it will last as long as possible.

Regular maintenance inspections will give you a chance to spot and take care of potential problems before leaks develop. For advice on inspections—and on dealing with leaks, should problems slip by you—see page 49. When the weather clears, use this chapter's advice on making repairs.

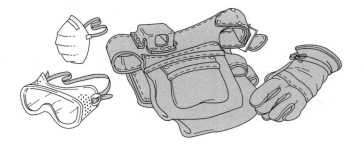

REPAIRING ASPHALT SHINGLES

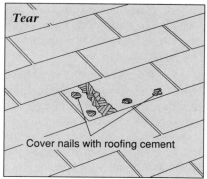

Liberally trowel plastic roofing cement under the tear. Press the shingle in place, then secure each side with roofing nails, covering the nailheads and the tear with roofing cement.

To flatten a curled shingle, apply plastic roofing cement under the lifted portion. Press shingle in place, then tack it down with roofing nails. Cover nailheads with cement.

Whether you repair or replace asphalt shingles depends on the type of damage they've sustained. Cracks, small holes, tears, and curled corners can usually be repaired with plastic roofing cement. But badly worn or damaged—or completely missing—shingles must be replaced.

REPLACING ASPHALT SHINGLES

Save any extra shingles when a new roof is installed so you will have replacements available if they're needed later. Otherwise, you'll have to find new shingles that match.

The illustrations below show how to replace shingles. Fasten the new shingles with galvanized roofing nails long enough (at least 1½ inches) to penetrate all roofing layers; seal nailheads with plastic roofing cement. Try to work so a shingle above will cover nailheads in the lower one.

Don't remove a damaged shingle that's on a ridge or along a hip; instead, nail each corner in place. Then apply plastic roofing cement to the underside of a new shingle and place it over the defective one. Nail each corner, then cover the nailheads with roofing cement.

REPAIRING ASPHALT SHINGLES

As shown in the drawings above, you can seal cracks and holes with plastic roofing cement by trowelling a liberal amount under the tear and securing the torn halves with roofing nails. You can also spread cement under a curled corner and press the corner in place; if necessary, tack it down with a roofing nail. Cover the nailhead with more cement.

Repair an asphalt roof on a warm day, when the shingles are more pliable; cold shingles are brittle and break more easily. The day before you plan to make repairs, store the can of roofing cement indoors, allowing it to reach room temperature so it will spread evenly.

HOW TO REPLACE AN ASPHALT SHINGLE

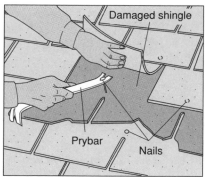

l) Lift the shingle tab above the damaged one and, with a prybar, remove both rows of nails holding the damaged shingle.

2) Slide the new shingle into place, taking care not to damage the roofing felt (snip the top corners if the shingle sticks).

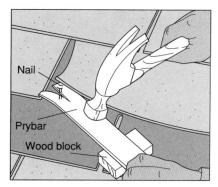

3) Nail on the new shingle. If you can't lift the tab above it high enough to nail underneath, use a prybar and hammer to tap it in.

REPAIRING ROLL & BUILT-UP ROOFING

Small repairs for built-up roofs and roofs covered with roll roofing are handled the same way. Leaks are most likely to develop at flashings (see page 93) or where blistered asphalt, cracks, holes, or separations between the roof surface and the drip edge have developed. Leaks usually show up directly below the problem area.

Small cracks can simply be filled with plastic roofing cement. Most other repairs involve clearing away gravel or wire-brushing the mineral surface around the problem, cutting out the damaged area, and applying a patch. You should be able to repair or even replace a roll-roofing roof using the installation instructions on page 79. A built-up roof is another story: if any hole is larger than about 1 square foot or if the roof is otherwise beyond repair, call a professional. It may make sense to replace it with one of the new single-ply roof products on the market.

When slicing through roofing or cutting out an area for a replacement patch, cut through only the defective layers. Squeeze out water and allow materials to dry by propping up the edges of the cut area. Cut a patch from either a piece of roll roofing or an asphalt shingle; secure it with plenty of plastic roofing cement and roofing nails, spaced 2 to 3 inches apart, as shown below.

HOW TO REPAIR A BLISTER

Cut blister with utility knife

1) Sweep all gravel aside, using a stiff-bristled broom. Then cut into the asphalt and the roofing felt with a utility knife to release the water and air under the blister.

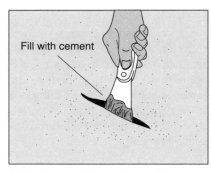

Fill with cement

2) With a putty knife, work roofing cement well under each edge of the cut. Cover the cut and an area 2 inches around all sides of it with a generous amount of the cement.

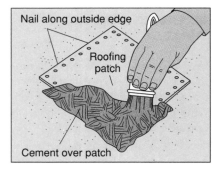

Nail along outside edge

Roofing patch

Cement over patch

3) Cut a patch of roofing 2 inches larger on all sides than the slit; press it into the roofing cement. Nail the patch down, then cover with more cement. Replace gravel when the cement starts to dry.

HOW TO PATCH A HOLE

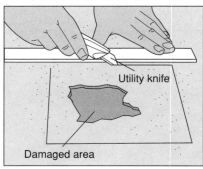

Utility knife

Damaged area

1) Sweep all gravel aside, using a stiff-bristled broom. Then cut out a rectangle around the damaged area. Remove damaged roofing. Cut a patch to fit the rectangle.

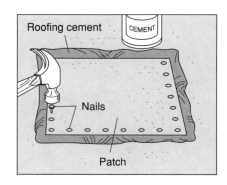

Roofing cement

CEMENT

Nails

Patch

2) Fill the rectangle with roofing cement, spreading it over the surrounding area. Nail the patch in place. Then cover the patch with more cement, spreading it 2 inches beyond the edges of the patch.

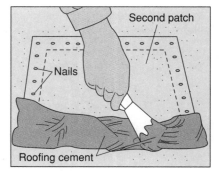

Second patch

Nails

Roofing cement

3) Cut a second patch 2 inches larger all around than the first. Nail it down and cover it with another coat of cement. Replace the gravel when the cement starts to dry.

REPLACING WOOD SHINGLES & SHAKES

As discussed on page 49, a good roof inspection can reveal whether any shingles or shakes are curled, broken, split, eroded, wind-lifted, or missing. The extent of the defects that you find will indicate whether or not you need to repair or replace roofing. If only a few shingles or shakes are split or wind-lifted, you can probably repair them. If any are badly splintered or curled, they should be replaced. If damage is extensive, you should consider replacing the entire roof.

If a shingle is split and the split doesn't line up with the joints between the shingles in the course above or below it, you should be able to leave it as it is. However, if the split occurs within an inch of the joints above or below its course, you'll need to remove and replace the shingle. Or you can cut a rectangle from 26-gauge flat sheet metal and drive it up under the split or damaged shingle (locate this metal piece where it will miss the nails holding the shingle).

To remove a shingle or shake, split it along the grain and pull out as much of the damaged wood as possible. Pry up the shingle or shake directly above the one you're removing in preparation for cutting the nails. Rent or buy a shingle ripper or use a hacksaw blade to cut off the nails flush with the sheathing, taking care not to penetrate the roofing felt. In order to use the ripper, you must slide it under the shingle and around a nail; then cut through the shank of the nail with a hammer blow (see illustration at top right). Remember that two sets of nails run through each shingle or shake—the set just above the butt line of the course above and the set above the butt line of the next higher course.

Trim a replacement to fit the space, using a roofer's hatchet or a saw. Leave a clearance (¼ inch for shingles, ⅜ to ½ inch for shakes) on each side of the replacement—room for the wood to expand when it gets wet. To secure the replacement shingle or shake, simply spread some plastic roofing cement or silicone caulking compound on the underside of its thinner section and carefully tap it into place with a hammer (protect the butt with a block of wood). Or you can blind-nail the shingle or shake, using the technique shown below.

HOW TO REPLACE A WOOD SHINGLE OR SHAKE

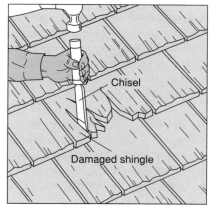

1) Carefully split the damaged shingle along the grain and pull out as much of it as possible. Pry up the shingles directly above the damaged one to reach the nails securing it.

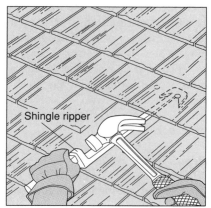

2) Cut the nails that secure the shingle to the roof deck, using a shingle ripper as shown (or saw nails off with a hacksaw blade). Don't damage sheathing or underlayment.

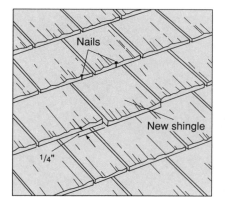

3) Insert the new shingle so it protrudes ¼ inch below adjoining shingles; allow a ⅜-inch clearance on each side. Drive in two roofing nails at an angle just below the edge of the row above.

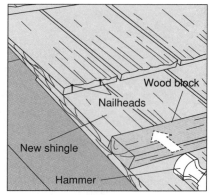

4) Drive the edge of the new shingle even with the others, using a hammer and wood block. As the nails bend, their heads will be pulled up under the shingles above.

REPAIRING TILE & METAL ROOFING

Most masonry tile and metal roofs last as long as the house, so problems with them are usually limited to leaks, broken tiles, and dented or damaged metal shingles or panels. Though you may be able to handle small patches or replacements, it's better to hire a professional roofer for major problems—particularly with ceramic tile, rounded concrete tile, and metal panel systems.

Repairing or replacing masonry tile. Small holes or cracks can be patched with plastic roofing cement. If the corner or butt of a masonry tile is cracked, clean the area with a wire brush and seal the crack with plastic roofing cement. If the crack extends above the overlap of the tile below, it's best to remove and replace the tile.

If you're replacing a tile on a roof where tiles have been laid directly on decking, the job is simple: gently pry up the appropriate tile or tiles in the course above the cracked one, remove the old tile pieces, spread a little roofing cement on the underside of the replacement tile, and slide the new tile into position.

If you're replacing tiles that are nailed to battens, use a hammer to break up the old tile. Remove as much of it as you can. Use a prybar to lift the tile or tiles directly above the broken one; and remove nails and any remaining shards with a shingle ripper, prybar, pliers, or wire cutters. Spread a little roofing cement on the underside of the replacement tile and slide it into position, hooking it over the batten (do not nail it).

Repairing and replacing metal shingles. Small holes in metal roofing can be patched like those in metal flashings (see the facing page). For large repairs or replacements, call a specialist in metal roofing.

If you have extra shingles that match the ones on your roof, study the method of interlock to understand what you need to do to remove and replace a shingle that's beyond repair. The chances are good that you'll need to cut the damaged shingle to remove it and modify interlocking edges to accommodate a new one. Be sure to protect underlayment beneath shingles and to seal joints with silicone caulking compound or plastic roofing cement.

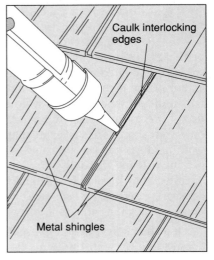

To replace a metal shingle, cut out the damaged one, then trim the edges of the replacement so it can be slipped into place and hooked to its mates. Seal seams with silicone or roofing cement.

HOW TO REPLACE MASONRY TILE

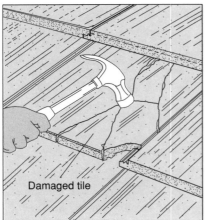

1) To remove a damaged tile, break it with a hammer and pull out the pieces. Be careful not to damage neighboring tiles.

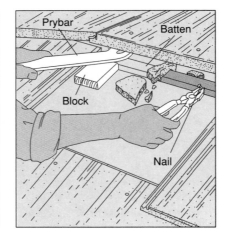

2) Using a prybar, carefully lift the tile directly above to remove shards of the broken one. Also pull up any protruding nails.

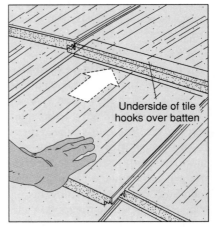

3) Slide the replacement tile under the interlocking edge of its neighbor and push it up under the tile above, hooking it onto the batten.

REPAIRING FLASHINGS

I f leaks show up around flashing, it's important to do repairs as soon as possible. Flashings are used where runoff could invade roof materials; a leak can funnel streams of water into your house.

Renail any loose nails and cover all exposed nailheads with plastic roofing cement. Plug pinholes with spots of roofing cement; patch holes up to a diameter of about ¾ inch with the same material as the damaged flashing. To do this, roughen the area around the hole with a wire brush or sandpaper, then wipe the flashing clean. Cut a patch of flashing material 2 inches larger than the hole on all sides. Apply roofing cement to the area; press the patch in place and hold it for several minutes. Cover the patch with another coat of cement.

Replace any flashing that has larger holes or is badly corroded. Buy new flashing or fashion it from aluminum or copper, using the old flashing as a pattern. Some types of flashing will slide into place directly over the old flashing. More likely, you'll have to remove several courses of shingles as well as the flashing itself—which may be better left to a professional roofer. Otherwise, refer to this book's instructions for installation of your type of roofing (and reverse the process to remove roofing).

To make flashing less visible, it can be painted to match the roof. Use a stiff brush and solvent to remove any flaking paint, rust, or corrosion from the flashing (keep solvent off asphalt shingles, or it will dissolve them). Apply a zinc-base primer, then spray on two or more light coats of rust-resistant metal paint.

Regularly check for any breaks in the all-important seals at the flashings' edges and reseal them.

FOUR FLASHING REPAIRS

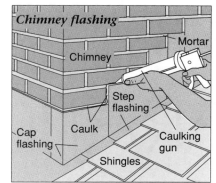

Chip out old mortar and caulking along cap flashing. Caulk joints between chimney and cap flashing and between cap and step flashings.

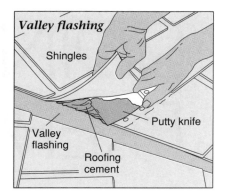

Lift edges of shingles along the flashing and spread roofing cement on flashing to about 6 inches in from the edges of the shingles.

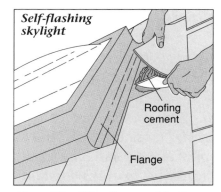

If possible, lift adjacent shingles and liberally spread roofing cement between the skylight flange and the roofing felt.

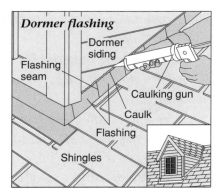

Remove any old caulk; apply new caulking compound between flashing and siding or shingles and between seams in flashing.

HOW TO REPLACE VENT PIPE FLASHING

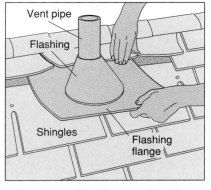

1) Remove shingles covering the flange at the back and sides; pull or cut the nails, lift off flashing, and clean the vent pipe.

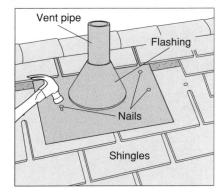

2) Position new flashing over the vent, nail where shingles will cover, seal nailheads with roofing cement, and replace shingles.

SIDING PREPARATION

If you're adding onto your home or building a new house, you'll be able to put sheathing and siding directly on new wall studs. But if you're re-siding, you'll have to either strip off the old material or apply new siding over it. This chapter will help you prepare for either treatment.

Which siding material is best for your situation? Consider the information on pages 28–47 when you're making this decision.

Can you handle the job yourself? Turn back to page 52 to review the specific skills and tools needed for siding work. And remember, the difficulty of putting on siding depends on which material you're using—some are much easier to work with than others. To get a clear idea of the procedures the material you've chosen requires, read through the installation chapter beginning on page 100.

If you've decided to do the work yourself, your next task is to estimate and order materials. The information on the facing page will guide you with this.

Then, materials at hand, it's time to prepare the walls.

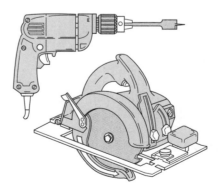

ESTIMATING YOUR NEEDS

Figuring the amount of siding needed to cover your house is usually just a matter of measuring exterior walls, calculating square footage, and adjusting the resulting figures for waste.

Gather a pad, pencil, and measuring tape. Depending upon how complex your house walls are, you can either make small sketches of the walls, noting their measurements, or simply list the dimensions for each wall. You might be able to avoid getting out a ladder to measure the height of a wall if you can measure the width of one board or the length of a shingle exposure and multiply this by the number of boards or courses from top to bottom.

Rounding off measurements to the nearest foot, divide the surfaces to be covered into rectangles and triangles (for wall sections beneath gables). To calculate the area of rectangles, multiply length by width. Most triangles will have two sides that join at something close to a right angle. Multiply the length of one of these sides by the other, then divide by 2 to approximate the area.

Add together all the areas you've computed. Then (except for sheet sidings, such as plywood), subtract the areas of windows, doors, chimneys, and other places the new siding will not cover. The result is approximately how many square feet of siding you'll need; add 10 percent for waste. If your house has steep angles at the gables or other architectural features that will necessitate a lot of cutting, add another 15 percent to the total amount you will need to order.

Siding materials are sold by the linear foot, square foot, board foot, or "square" (a roofing term for the amount needed to cover 100 square feet, allowing for overlap). Here's how to estimate each material.

Board sidings (including plywood and hardboard lap sidings) are usually sold by the board foot or by the linear foot. Calculate the number of board feet (l inch by 12 inches by 12 inches) or linear feet required to cover the necessary square footage.

Be sure to take into account the overlap of most board sidings. You'll need about 1,240 square feet of 8-inch horizontal bevel siding, for example, to cover 1,000 square feet of wall space. Manufacturers offer charts to help estimate your needs, based on their specific patterns.

Vinyl and aluminum sidings are usually sold by the number of square feet a given amount covers. When ordering, you must also estimate how many linear feet of various trim pieces you'll need.

Shingles and shakes provide coverage that depends on the exposure you use and whether you are installing single or double courses (see page 108). Both materials are sold by the square.

Because greater exposures are allowed on walls than on roofs, a square may cover more than 100 square feet of a wall. The table below will help you determine the actual coverage you'll get with various exposures of shingles and shakes (single courses).

Plywood and hardboard sheets are sold in sizes that correlate directly with square footage. Add 10 percent for normal waste and—if your house has sharply angled walls—another 15 percent for extra cutting.

Additional materials may be needed, depending upon the siding and the type of construction; these might include sheathing, insulation, building paper or house wrap, or furring strips. And you will need flashing, trim, and nails. To figure your requirements, read through the instructions this chapter offers on preparation and installation for each material.

APPROXIMATE COVERAGE PROVIDED BY ONE SQUARE OF SHINGLES OR SHAKES
(in square feet)

Exposure	5½"	7½"	8½"	10"	11½"
Shingle lengths					
16"	110	150	170	200	230
18"	100	136	154	181	209
24"	73	100	113	133	153
Shake lengths & types					
18" hand-split	55	75	85	100	—
24" hand-split	55	75	85	100	115
18" straight-split	65	90	100	—	—
24" straight-split	65	75	85	100	115

PREPARING THE WALLS

Regardless of the type of siding you're using, you'll want to fasten it to a solid base. When you're applying siding to new construction, the studs—and sheathing, when necessary—make a suitable base. If you're siding over an existing wall that is flat and sound, you may be able to nail new siding directly over it, avoiding substantial work, mess, and weather exposure. On the other hand, if the existing siding is metal, vinyl, or masonry, or is bumpy and irregular, you'll either have to strip it off or provide a nailing base of furring strips on top of it.

REMOVING EXISTING SIDING

If you must remove existing siding, equip yourself with a claw hammer, a flat prybar, and a chisel. A pair of locking pliers is useful for pulling nails in hard-to-reach places. A "cat's paw" nail puller—a special prying device—is very handy for lifting nails quickly but can mar wood. If you're removing wood siding that you intend to save and reuse, gently detach the siding from the studs or sheathing with a flat prybar and then pull the nails, protecting the surface with a scrap block.

As you remove materials, pull or bend over nails and stack materials neatly to keep the work site safe.

Wood boards. Board-and-batten siding is easy to strip. Simply pry up each batten to raise the nailheads. Pull the nails and remove the battens, then remove the boards.

For lap sidings (both plywood and hardboard types), start at the top of the wall and pry off the top molding. Then you'll have easy access to the nails on each successive layer of boards as you work down to the bottom.

For boards with mitered edges that are face-nailed, use a nail puller to lift the nails until you can remove them with a claw hammer. If you want to avoid marring the wood, use the nail puller on the first board and then raise nails from subsequent boards with a prybar.

To remove tongue-and-groove boards that are blind-nailed through the tongue, first take off the molding and pull any visible nails from the top board on a horizontal board wall or the end board on a vertical board wall. Then work your way down or back, using a nail puller or prybar to raise the nails from each tongue.

Vinyl and aluminum. For horizontal panels, start by removing the molding that covers the top row of nails. Using a prybar or nail puller, lift the panel and loosen the nails. Then remove the nails from each panel, slip out the interlocking device at its bottom edge, and expose the nails for the next panel. Work your way down to the ground.

For vertical panels, start where the nails of an end panel are concealed by molding. Remove the molding, loosen and remove the nails, and unlock the panel. Work sideways along the wall.

Shingles and shakes. Use a square-bottom shovel to pry shingles and shakes from the wall. Simply insert the shovel underneath the shingles or shakes, lift them up, and pull them off. It's usually easiest to start at the top and work down the wall. Pull any remaining nails.

Plywood and hardboard panels. With a prybar or a nail puller, you can lift the nails holding plywood or hardboard sheets around the perime- ter and along studs. When you have most of the nails lifted, pry the sheets loose.

Stucco. Removing stucco is hard work; if at all possible, apply new siding over the top. For an extensive removal job, you would do well to call in a demolition contractor. To do the work yourself, you'll need a cold chisel and a heavyweight hammer (or rent an electric or pneumatic hammer). Be sure to wear goggles when you work.

Asbestos-cement shingles. Because of cancer risks associated with airborne asbestos particles, this material should only be removed by an asbestos-abatement contractor. The Environmental Protection Agency (EPA) and the Consumer Product Safety Commission (CPSA) recommend leaving inert asbestos alone unless it's friable—flaking or crumbling. For your state and local regulations, contact public health agencies. Some experts recommend leaving asbestos shingles in place and covering them over with vinyl or aluminum siding.

SHEATHING THE WALLS

Before the finished siding is applied, most new walls receive some type of sheathing to strengthen them, serve as a nailing base for siding, and/or boost insulation. Existing walls usually don't require sheathing unless you're stripping off the old siding and applying a different type that calls for it. Check the siding manufacturer's directions and local codes to determine whether sheathing is required or suggested in your case.

Sheathings are of two sorts, structural and nonstructural.

Structural sheathing. Structural sheathings are an integral part of the house's framing. They tie together wall studs, contributing shear strength and rigidity and forming a solid nailing base for siding materials. Most structural sheathings don't add much insulation value.

Though solid boards were once commonly used for structural sheathing, less expensive, more effective panel products have all but eliminated them from use. Today's most common structural sheathings are plywood, oriented strand board (OSB), and waferboard. Exterior gypsum board is another structural sheathing, often chosen for use in commercial construction because of its resistance to fire.

When choosing plywood, OSB, or waferboard panels, be sure they are rated as wall sheathing. And choose an appropriate thickness. Although you can use panels as thin as ⁵⁄₁₆ inch for some applications, it's usually a good idea to spend a little bit more for sturdier ½-inch panels.

The most common panel size is 4 by 8 feet; you can get some products in 4- by 9- and 4- by 10-foot sheets.

Using 6-penny galvanized nails, fasten panels (usually horizontally) to wall studs, spacing nails 6 inches apart along the panels' edges and 12 inches apart mid-panel (or as specified by codes). Allow an expansion gap of ¹⁄₁₆ inch between panel ends and ⅛ inch between panel edges.

Nonstructural sheathing. Nonstructural sheathings don't add significantly to a wall's strength but can greatly increase it's insulation value.

Rigid foam and cellulose-fiber panels are generally used to sheath walls that don't require strengthening (though some types of cellulose fiberboard can be used as structural sheathing). These materials may be attached directly to wall studs or masonry walls, under or over structural sheathing (depending upon nailing requirements), or—in some cases—

over existing siding before re-siding. Your building materials supplier can offer advice appropriate for your particular circumstances.

The two most common types of foam board sheathing are made of polyisocyanurate or extruded polystyrene. Polyisocyanurate has higher per-inch insulation (R) values—up to R-8.7 per inch—than polystyrene, though its value decreases when it's punctured by nails. For more on R-values, see page 72.

Foam board thicknesses range from ⅜ inch to 4¼ inches. For covering existing siding, ½-inch and ¾-inch thicknesses are commonly used. Standard panels are 2 by 8, 4 by 8, and 4 by 9 feet, though some foam can be purchased in fan-folded panels that run up to 50 feet long. Most panels have square edges meant to be butted together; some have shiplap or tongue-and-groove edges.

Foam panels come plain or with either reflective aluminum or matte facings. Which type to choose—and which side to face outward—depends upon your wall's makeup and the siding you're applying. As a rule, use foil-faced panels beneath brick, stucco, and some wood sidings. Non-foil-faced panels are generally recommended beneath aluminum, vinyl, and wood-based sidings.

Fire codes and safety may affect how nonstructural panels are applied. Despite the fact that foil facings help reduce the combustibility of nonstructural sheathing panels, these products should not be left exposed—be sure to follow manufacturer's instructions in this regard. Foam and cellulose panels can feed a fire, and foam, in particular, can give off toxic smoke if ignited.

Most foam and cellulose panels are extremely lightweight and can be cut with a utility knife. Nail the panels to wall studs with large-headed galvanized nails that are long enough to penetrate studs at least 1 inch. Space nails according to manufactur-

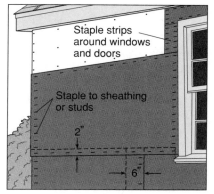

Staple strips around windows and doors

Staple to sheathing or studs

2"

6"

er's instructions (because these panels are not structural, 12-inch spacing is usually sufficient). Drive nails flush, being careful not to crush the panels with your final hammer blow.

APPLYING BUILDING PAPER

Building paper is like roofing felt. A black felt or kraft paper impregnated with asphalt, it is applied between the sheathing (or the unsheathed studs) and the siding to resist wind and water without trapping moist air. It comes in rolls 36 to 40 inches wide and long enough to cover 200 to 500 square feet (allowing for overlap).

Though some building codes require the use of building paper, it isn't always mandatory. You may want to apply it anyway if your siding will be subjected to heavy winds or to wind-driven rain or snow, or if it consists of boards or shingles that present numerous places for wind and water to penetrate.

Apply building paper in horizontal strips, starting at the bottom of each wall and working up. Overlap 2 inches at horizontal joints and 6 inches at vertical joints. Wrap the paper at least 12 inches around each corner. To cut it, use a utility knife. Staple or nail the paper to studs or sheathing, using just enough fasteners to hold it in place until siding is installed.

INSTALLING HOUSE WRAP

It's estimated that more than 20 percent of the heat loss from a house is caused by air infiltration—the entrance of drafts blowing in through tiny cracks and the loss of heated air to the outside. To protect against this, many builders now apply house wrap before installing siding. House wrap is a spun-bonded or woven polymer material that keeps water and drafts out, yet "breathes" so it doesn't trap moisture in the walls.

House wrap comes in 8-foot-wide rolls and is easy and quick to install. On a still day when you have a helper, start at one corner of the house and, holding the roll vertically, unroll about 6 feet of the material. Let it overlap the corner about 12 inches, and fasten it in place there with "cap nails" (roofing nails that have a plastic or metal washer-type head). Make sure that the material is plumb and that the bottom edge aligns with the foundation line. Secure the material every 12 to 18 inches along studs (most types of house wrap have stud lines marked on the fabric—just align the first one and the others should automatically fall on subsequent studs).

Unroll the material right over window and door openings. When you've finished a wall, go back and cut an X-shape from corner to corner in those openings. Then, fold back the resulting triangular flaps, staple them to studs around the perimeter of the opening, and cut off the excess. Continue around the perimeter and lap the final corner. If you need more than one width of wrap to cover a wall, lap the upper sheet over the lower one about 2 inches. Seal any seams with special tape that's made to be used with house wrap.

ATTACHING FURRING STRIPS

If your present siding is masonry or is bumpy and irregular, you may need to install a base of furring strips, generally a gridwork of 1 by 3 boards or strips, placed to provide nailing support for the new siding at appropriate intervals.

Use a long, straight board or taut line to determine where it is necessary to shim furring strips in order to create a flat plane. To shim, tap wood shingles between the wall and furring strips. Check furring strips for plumb before you nail them in place, and adjust if necessary.

Secure the strips every 12 inches with nails long enough to penetrate studs at least 1 inch. If the existing walls are masonry, use concrete nails or masonry anchors.

PREPARING WINDOWS & DOORS

Unless you strip the walls first, new siding will add to the thickness of your walls. For both weatherproofing and appearance, it's usually necessary to build up the jambs and sills of windows and doors to compensate for the added thickness. (For synthetic sidings, special add-on trim pieces are provided to handle this.)

Gently pry off the old exterior trim and set the pieces aside. Extend wood jambs by adding small wood strips to them as shown on the facing page at bottom left. Cut extenders the same width as the jambs and as deep as the new siding (including sheathing and furring as well as the exterior material).

For each window and door, cut the first extender to fit across the top and glue and nail it in place. Then butt side jamb extenders up against it and cut their lower ends at the angle needed to match the sill. Fill any gaps between old and new with wood putty or vinyl spackling compound and sand flush.

LAYOUTS FOR FURRING WALLS

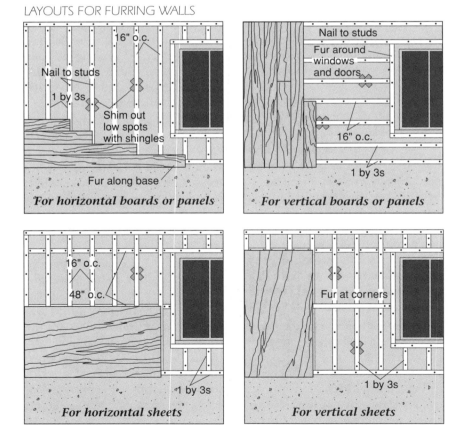

For horizontal boards or panels

For vertical boards or panels

For horizontal sheets

For vertical sheets

FLASHING SIDING

Flashing protects walls the same way it protects roofs (see page 64)—by preventing water that runs down a wall from penetrating the joints between materials. Standard galvanized and aluminum flashing is available at home-improvement centers. Types made for vinyl and metal sidings are sold by siding manufacturers. Specialty flashings and flashings made of copper are usually custom-fabricated at sheet-metal shops.

Use galvanized nails for galvanized flashings, aluminum nails for aluminum flashings, bronze nails for copper flashings—combining differing metals can cause corrosive electrolysis that may weaken nails and stain siding.

The drawings at top right show two standard types of siding flashing—drip caps and Z flashing. If you're siding where a wall meets a roof, also review dormer flashings on page 67.

Drip caps. Before applying any type of siding, be sure that drip caps are placed over windows and doors. These L-shaped or Z-shaped metal flashings extend from under the siding out over the window and door frames. Cut these with tin snips and nail them in place over windows and doors, positioning nails where siding will cover them.

Z flashing. Along horizontal joints between large sheets of plywood or hardboard, Z-shaped flashings are often necessary. After installing the lower sheet, fit Z flashing along its upper edge and nail to studs or sheathing. Cover the flashing's upper flange with the bottom edge of the next sheet of siding.

ESTABLISHING A BASE LINE

No matter what siding you use, you'll have to align its lowest edge along the base of each wall by snapping a level chalk line no less than 8 inches above grade (ground level). When applying new siding over old, the line is usually set 1 inch below the lower edge of the existing siding.

WORKING WITH FLASHING

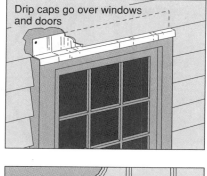

Drip caps go over windows and doors

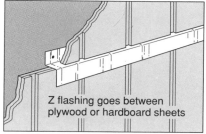

Z flashing goes between plywood or hardboard sheets

Excavate any surrounding soil that interferes with this 8-inch clearance, sloping the grade away from the house so water won't pool by the foundation. You may find it necessary to "step" the siding—adjust the base line up or down—to conform to a hillside or irregular grade. If you're applying horizontal siding, shingles, or shakes, work out the sizes of the required steps so they correspond with the planned exposure for each course.

If you have no helper, stretch the chalk line from a concrete nail pounded into the foundation wall (one at each end if necessary).

EXTENDING A JAMB

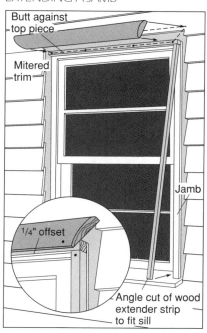

Butt against top piece

Mitered trim

Jamb

1/4" offset

Angle cut of wood extender strip to fit sill

EXTENDING A SILL

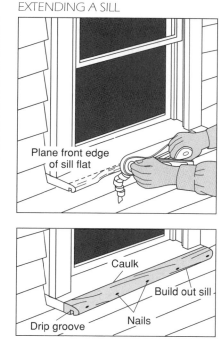

Plane front edge of sill flat

Caulk

Build out sill

Drip groove

Nails

SNAPPING A CHALK LINE

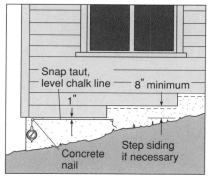

Snap taut, level chalk line

8" minimum

1"

Concrete nail

Step siding if necessary

SIDING INSTALLATION

After you've handled the preparatory steps, you're ready for the gratifying part of the job: installing the siding. This is the stage when your efforts show results.

This chapter offers step-by-step techniques for installing board sidings, some types of vinyl and aluminum systems, shingles and shakes, and plywood and hardboard siding panels. Because the skills needed for installing steel and other sheet-metal panel systems, stucco and related materials, and brick and stone veneers are beyond the talents of most homeowners, installation of these is not covered here.

Remember that the guidelines are general and may need to be modified to fit a particular situation. Pay attention to local codes. And if you encounter a discrepancy between the installation method recommended by your siding's manufacturer and advice given here, follow the manufacturer's instructions.

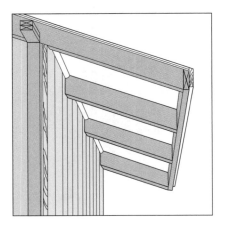

APPLYING BOARD SIDING

For the sake of simplicity, all solid board siding patterns are grouped into this single category. But for proper installation, you must treat each basic pattern individually.

The chart on page 102 will tell you whether a particular pattern is applied vertically or horizontally, as well as the type of backing it requires, the size of nail to use, and the correct technique for nailing. Apply board sidings over building paper.

In addition to the solid board sidings discussed in the chart, you can buy plywood or hardboard lap sidings. These materials are installed using methods similar to those for solid wood bevel siding. (Though the drawing below right shows face-nailed hardboard siding, some types are blind-nailed.)

Before you begin nailing up siding boards, let the wood acclimate to local humidity. (Store boards flat, raised above the ground on blocks or scraps.) Then prime or prefinish sides, edges, and (during installation) cut ends. Next, figure out how you want to treat the corners. Typical treatments for both inside and outside corners are illustrated above right.

When working out your layout, try to plan rows so boards are set seamlessly around windows, doors, and other openings. With horizontal siding, a slight adjustment to your base line may do the trick. If you must butt board ends together, stagger the joints.

Nailing. Nail each board individually —don't nail through overlapping parts. Use stainless-steel, high-tensile-

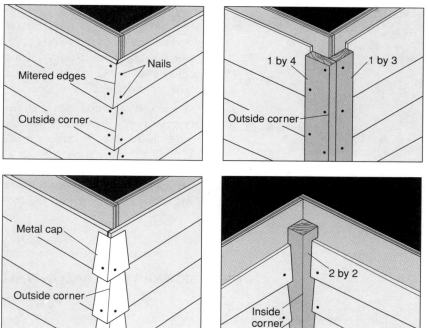

strength aluminum or hot-dipped galvanized siding or box nails to face-nail, or similar casing nails to blind-nail. Spiral or ring-shank nails offer the best holding power.

The nail sizes in the chart on page 102 are for new construction. When putting siding over an existing wall, choose nails that penetrate

studs at least 1¼ inch. As shown in the chart, 6-inch-wide and narrower patterns require only one nail per bearing; some wider boards require two. If boards tend to split, try blunting the nail tips with a hammer; otherwise, predrill nail holes, using a drill bit that is slightly smaller than the nails' diameter.

PLYWOOD LAP SIDING

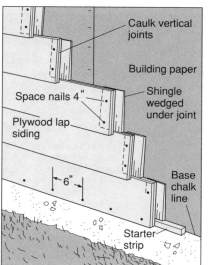

HARDBOARD LAP SIDING

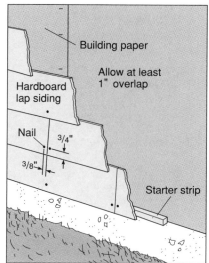

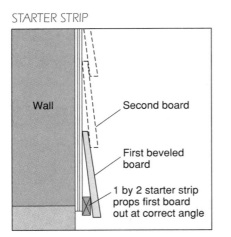

First board. With horizontal siding, the first board goes at the bottom. Most types require a 1 by 2 starter strip beneath the board's lower edge, along the wall's base, to push the first board out so it will match the angle of the other boards.

For vertical wood siding, begin at one corner of the house. If you intend to install closed cornices as explained on the facing page, put in 2-by-2 blocking (see drawing on the facing page, bottom right). Align one edge of the first board with the cor-ner and check its other edge for plumb. Adjust as necessary; then trim the outside edge with a plane or saw until it fits the corner. Be sure the board's lower end is flush with your base chalk line, and nail it in place.

Successive boards. To lay out horizontal board siding, you'll need a "story pole." As shown on page 108, make the story pole from a 1 by 2 that's as long as your tallest wall's height (unless that wall is more than one story). Starting at one end, mark

BOARD SIDING: TYPES AND INSTALLATION

Type	Direction	Backing	Nailing instructions
Board on board / Board and batten	Vertical only	Solid sheathing or blocking or furring on 24" centers	Allow ½"–1" overlap. Use 8d nails for underboards, 10d for overboards. Nail 6" and narrower boards once per bearing; nail 8" overboards twice, 3"–4" apart, at center.
Clapboard	Horizontal only	Solid sheathing or studs or furring on 24" centers	Allow 1" overlap; face-nail 1½" from bottom edge (½" above edge of lower piece) with 10d nails, once per bearing.
Bevel, Bungalow	Horizontal only	Solid sheathing or studs or furring on 24" centers	Allow 1" overlap; face-nail 1½" from bottom edge (½" above edge of lower piece) with 8d nails, once per bearing.
Dolly Varden	Horizontal only	Solid sheathing or studs or furring on 24" centers	Allow 1" overlap; face-nail ½" from bottom edge (½" above edge of lower piece) with 10d nails, once per bearing. Allow ⅛" expansion gap at overlap.
Tongue and groove / Tongue-and-groove drop	Horizontal or vertical	Solid sheathing or studs or furring or blocking on 24" centers	Blind-nail 6" and narrower boards once per bearing with 8d nails. Face-nail wider boards with first nail 1" above bottom edge, second nail 3"–4" above first.
Channel rustic / Shiplap drop	Horizontal or vertical	Solid sheathing or studs or furring or blocking on 24" centers	Face-nail 6" and narrower boards once per bearing, 1" above bottom edge with 8d nails; with wider boards use second nail 3"–4" above first.
Log cabin	Horizontal or vertical	Solid sheathing or studs or furring or blocking on 24" centers	Face-nail 6" and narrower boards once per bearing, 1½" above bottom edge with 10d nails; with wider boards, use two nails per bearing, 3"–4" apart.

BEVELING FOR FIT

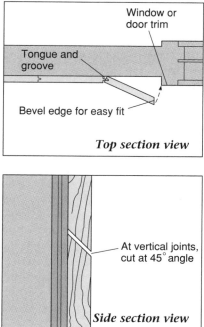

Window or door trim

Tongue and groove

Bevel edge for easy fit

Top section view

At vertical joints, cut at 45° angle

Side section view

the pole at intervals equaling the width of the siding boards.

Hold or tack the story pole flush with the base line, then transfer the marks to each corner and to the trim at each window and door casing.

Apply the boards from bottom to top. Unless the chart on the facing page calls for overlapping or spacing, fit the boards tightly together.

Where vertical boards join end to end, cut the ends of the boards at a 45-degree angle, sloping them to

ensure proper water runoff. Brush water repellent on board ends.

Corners and top of walls. To fit a shiplap or tongue-and-groove board into a corner or against a door or window frame, first rip it to the proper width. Then bevel the back edge that will fit against the frame; this will make it easier to push the board into place. When installing horizontal siding, determine whether the cornice will be open or closed (see below) before nailing the last board in place at the top of the wall.

To match the slope of a roofline, measure the angle with a T bevel. Transfer the angle to each board end, then cut (see drawing at right).

Open and closed cornices. Cornices are sometimes left open with wood-board siding—so the boards extend to the tops of the rafters, as shown below left. For this method, notch board ends where they intersect rafters and caulk them well after they're in place. Trim along the top edge, between rafters, using quarter-round molding or a narrow trim board (called a "frieze board").

If you prefer a closed cornice, you can buy or make a special wood board called a "plowed fascia board." This board, nailed over the rafter ends or existing fascia, has a routed groove near one edge for holding sof-

TRANSFERRING AN ANGLE

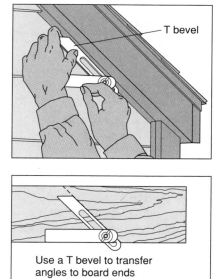

T bevel

Use a T bevel to transfer angles to board ends

fit boards or panels, as shown in the drawing below center.

To complete a closed cornice, mark both ends of the wall level with the top of the groove in the plowed fascia board. Snap a chalk line between the marks. For soffit boards that run perpendicular to the eaves (toward the wall), block above the chalk line with 2 by 2s to provide a place to nail ends of soffit boards, as shown below right. Nail boards to blocking; then caulk along the plowed fascia. For soffit boards that run along the length of the cornice, install blocking as shown below center.

CORNICES

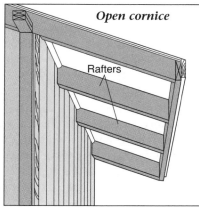

Open cornice

Rafters

Closed cornice

Blocking

Soffit

Caulk

Soffit vents

Plowed fascia board

Horizontal siding

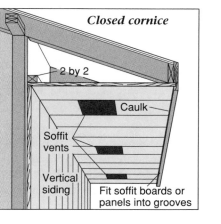

Closed cornice

2 by 2

Caulk

Soffit vents

Vertical siding

Fit soffit boards or panels into grooves

APPLYING VINYL & METAL SIDINGS

Vinyl, aluminum, and steel sidings are sold as complete systems that include not only the siding panels but all necessary attachment strips, trim, and related parts and pieces. Because the materials are lightweight and easy to cut and nail, some vinyl and aluminum systems can be homeowner-installed; steel siding, however, is better left to professionals.

As discussed on pages 38–43, both vinyl and aluminum systems come in a range of panel sizes made for either horizontal or vertical installation.

GENERAL TIPS

Nearly all manufacturers supply installation instructions for their products. Be sure to pick up a guide when you buy your siding.

As you'll see in the following paragraphs, techniques for installing vinyl and aluminum sidings are almost identical.

Backing. The backing must be smooth enough for the panels to lie flat. To be assured of such a surface, you'll need either smooth sheathing over wall studs or furring strips nailed to the butts of lap siding. A popular backing for vinyl and aluminum siding is ⅜-inch foam board insulation.

Tools. Most of the tools required are the same types needed for basic carpentry jobs—hammer, utility knife, carpenter's square, level, measuring tape, and so forth. In addition, you'll need tin snips or aviation shears for cutting and shaping the vinyl or aluminum.

Other helpful tools for vinyl include a snap-lock punch, which can punch connecting ears on the edges of siding used along the top or finishing courses, and a nail-hole punch, which produces elongated holes for nailing cut pieces. A power circular saw equipped with a fine-toothed blade (12 to 16 teeth per inch) can greatly speed cutting—some installers recommend mounting the blade in the reverse direction (only for cutting vinyl).

For cutting aluminum, you can use tin snips or a circular saw fitted with a fine-toothed blade. Be sure to wear eye protection when using any power saw, and wear a long-sleeved shirt and gloves to protect your arms and hands from slivers when cutting aluminum.

For bending aluminum, you can rent a brake from a tool-rental company. This allows you to bend siding so it conforms to corners and window and fascia trim. The brake is usually also used to make finishing trim from aluminum coil stock.

Nails and nailing. With vinyl siding, use aluminum, galvanized steel, or other corrosion-resistant nails. For aluminum siding, use only aluminum nails. The nails, with ⅛-inch shanks and heads at least 5⁄16 inch in diameter, should be long enough to penetrate solid backing at least ¾ inch. As a rule, you can choose 1½-inch nails for general use and trim and 2-inch nails for re-siding. Longer nails may be needed for going through insulation board into studs.

The two most important things to remember when nailing either vinyl or aluminum panels are: 1) unless otherwise specified, always nail in the center of nailing slots, and 2) never drive nails in too tightly—you want to hang panels from nails, not nail them fast.

Tolerances. These materials expand and contract significantly as they warm and cool. When cutting and attaching vinyl, figure it will expand ¼ inch per 10-foot length; aluminum will expand 1⁄16 to ⅛ inch. If you're installing these materials in cold weather, allow another ⅛ inch. These tolerances are averages—adjust them as necessary.

Cutting. A radial-arm saw or a circular saw with a fine-toothed blade (mounted in the reverse direction for vinyl) works best. Tin snips or aviation shears are better for small or irregular cuts. Or you can simply score a cut with a utility knife and snap a section of the siding material off by bending it back and forth. Corner posts and heavy trim are easier to cut with a hacksaw.

HANDLING CORNERS & TRIM

With aluminum and vinyl systems, the trim is installed first—around the house base line and window and door frames, and against soffit or gable edges—and panels are then fitted into it.

Installing corner posts. Install posts at inside and outside corners, allowing ¼ inch (vinyl) or ⅛ inch (aluminum) for expansion at the upper trim line and running the posts down to the base chalk line (see page 99).

Position each post by driving two nails through the top of the uppermost slots; the post should hang from the nails. Use a level to check for vertical alignment, and make any necessary adjustments.

Fasten the posts to the wall with nails every 12 inches. If you must stack one corner post above another, trim ¼ inch from the nailing flange at the bottom end of the top post. Then mount the top post so it overlaps the lower one by 1 inch.

TYPICAL VINYL OR ALUMINUM SIDING SYSTEM

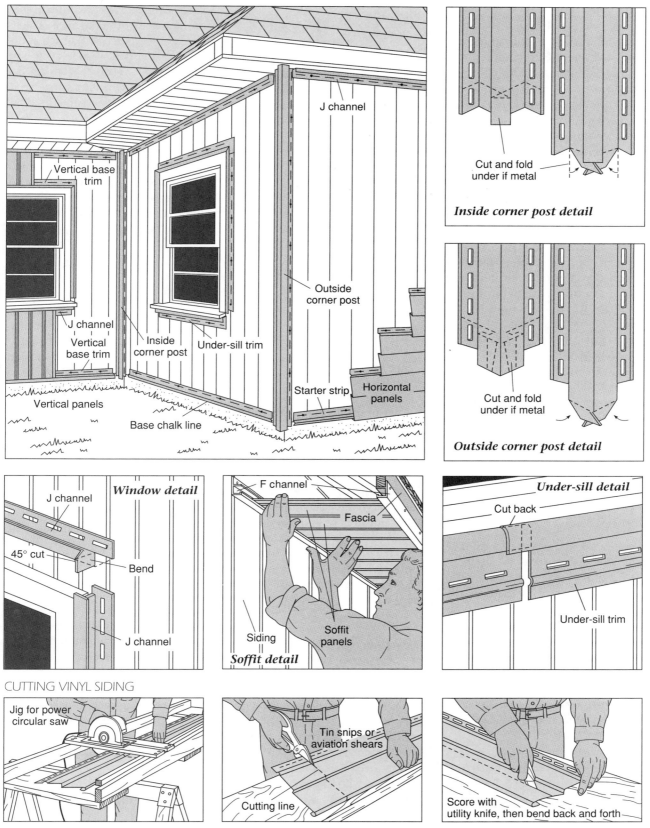

J channel

Vertical base trim

J channel

Vertical base trim

Inside corner post

Under-sill trim

Outside corner post

Starter strip

Horizontal panels

Vertical panels

Base chalk line

Inside corner post detail

Cut and fold under if metal

Outside corner post detail

Cut and fold under if metal

Window detail

J channel

45° cut

Bend

J channel

Soffit detail

F channel

Fascia

Siding

Soffit panels

Under-sill detail

Cut back

Under-sill trim

CUTTING VINYL SIDING

Jig for power circular saw

Tin snips or aviation shears

Cutting line

Score with utility knife, then bend back and forth

Installing starter strip or vertical base trim. Install the starter strip (for horizontal siding) or vertical base trim (for vertical siding) along the base chalk line. (With aluminum, this strip may be the same for either direction.)

Align the upper edge of the base trim with the chalk line and nail every 6 inches. When you come to an outside corner, allow ¼ inch (vinyl) or ⅛ inch (aluminum) for expansion between the starter strip or base trim and corner post.

Installing door and window trim. Your next step is to mount strips of appropriate trim—usually J channel, vertical base, or under-sill trim—around window and door openings. To reduce moisture and air flow, however, first run a bead of caulk around the openings, forming a seal. (If you intend to put vinyl covers on window sills and casings, do that before installing accessory trim.)

When you install door and window trim, do the top first, then the sides, and finally the under-sill trim.

Aluminum fittings are often folded, while vinyl is not. Aluminum J fittings around windows, for example, are often bent for a tight fit.

Along tops of doors and windows, install J-channel trim if you're using horizontal siding, vertical base trim if you're using vertical panels. Use lengths of trim that measure two channel widths longer than the top of the opening; either miter the ends or cut tabs at each end. Nail 12 inches on center.

Along the sides, use mitered trim if the top trim is mitered. When fitting side pieces, position the top nail at the top of the nailing slot, but drive remaining nails every 12 inches in the slots' centers.

To avoid problems fitting horizontal panels into narrow places (between adjacent windows, for example), fasten down the trim along only one side of such areas. Trim on the

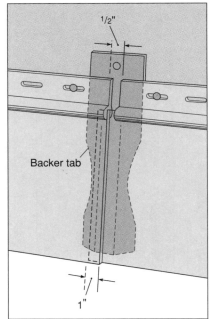

1/2"

Backer tab

1"

other side can be fastened as panels are put in place.

Under windows, install under-sill trim for horizontal siding, J-channel trim for vertical. Add furring strips where necessary to maintain the slope of siding.

Installing trim under eaves and rakes. If you're installing horizontal siding, use under-sill trim at the soffit and at the gable rake (remove existing rake molding first). For vertical panels, use J-channel trim. Nail 12 inches on center. Add furring strips if needed.

WORKING WITH HORIZONTAL PANELS

Allowing for expansion (¼ inch for vinyl, ⅛ inch for aluminum) where the panel fits into the J channel, fit and securely lock the starter panel into the starter strip. If you are installing the insulating backerboard that comes with some sidings, drop it behind the panel, with its beveled edge down and toward the wall.

Fitting end joints. Where panels meet, overlap the ends 1 inch. Run overlaps away from the most obvious focal point on each wall—such as the front walk or porch—so joints will be less obtrusive. When overlapping, cut 1½ inches of the nailing flange away from the end of one panel to allow for expansion.

Some vinyl and most aluminum horizontal sidings use backer tabs at joints to make the material more stable over long spans. Slip the backer tabs, flat side out, behind the joints as shown in the drawing at left.

Try to offset the joints at least 24 inches from one course to the next so vertical seams don't line up.

Fitting panels around windows and doors. You'll need a sharp knife, tin snips, or a power saw (for insulated siding) to trim panels to fit around windows and doors. Remember, though, to use either the saw or knife—never the tin snips—to cut the locking detail at the lower edge of the panel.

Measure window and door openings and cut panels to fit, allowing ¼ inch (for vinyl) or ⅛ inch (for aluminum) for expansion. Before fitting cut vinyl panels to under-sill trim, use a snap-lock punch to crimp nubs or "ears" along the trimmed edge. The ears, spaced 6 to 8 inches apart, should face outward so they can hook onto the under-sill trim.

With aluminum siding, gutter seal adhesive holds panels under windowsills and at soffits, especially where there is no other means of support. The gutter seal serves the same purpose as the ears crimped on vinyl.

To fit horizontal panels into narrow places, slip each panel into the trim along one side; as successive panels go into place, nail down the trim along the other side.

Installing top panels at eaves or gables. Measure from the bottom of the top lock to the eaves and subtract

¼ inch (for vinyl) or ⅛ inch (for aluminum) for expansion. To determine the width of the final horizontal panel, measure in several places along the eaves.

Cut the panel as needed, and use the snap-lock punch to crimp ears along its upper edge every 6 to 8 inches. Then tuck the panel into the trim.

At the gables, cut panels at an angle to fit into the J channels, F channels, or quarter-round moldings along the gable rake. Crimp ears as for window trim.

HANDLING VERTICAL PANELS

Once the corner posts and trim are in, locate the center of each wall and, using a level and a straightedge, draw a line down the center. Allowing ¼ inch (for vinyl) or ⅛ inch (for aluminum) for expansion at the top, center the first panel over the line. Fasten it every 8 inches with nails positioned at the top of the nailing slots.

Working from this starter panel, install successive panels. These

VERTICAL-PANEL DOOR & WINDOW TREATMENT

Vertical panel
½" J channel
Window or door frame

Vertical panel
Under-sill trim
½" J channel
Window or door frame

should be long enough to fit between the trim strips, minus ¼ inch (for vinyl) or ⅛ inch (for aluminum) for expansion. Panels should rest on the vertical base trim at the base.

Insert each panel into the J channel along the top of the wall. Letting it rest on the vertical base trim, lock it into the previous panel.

Nails for successive panels should be positioned in the slot centers, spaced every 8 to 16 inches (de-

pending on the manufacturer's recommendation).

When fitting vertical panels around windows and doors, follow instructions for "Working with Horizontal Panels" (preceding).

Before you insert the last panels into the corner posts, install J or U channels or under-sill trim in the corner post slots (manufacturers' instructions vary). You may want to raise the J channels with 5/16-inch shims (for ½-inch J channels) to keep panels on the same plane.

Then, as illustrated at left, insert uncut panel edges (and cut edges near V grooves) into the J channel. Cut edges of flat sections should be inserted between the J channel and the post's outer flange.

SPECIAL SITUATIONS

Vinyl siding systems can include fascia trim, window trim, and other specialty parts that give a finished look. The installation of these—as well as soffit panel application and the handling of transitions between horizontal and vertical panels—varies from one manufacturer to another. For details on your particular system, consult the manufacturer's recommendations.

MARKING PANELS
AT EAVES

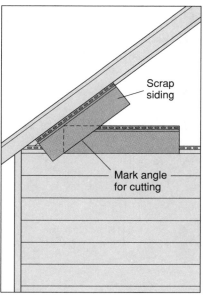

Scrap siding

Mark angle for cutting

VERTICAL-PANEL
CORNER TREATMENT

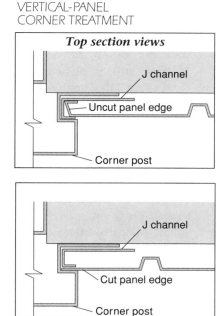

Top section views

J channel
Uncut panel edge
Corner post

J channel
Cut panel edge
Corner post

APPLYING SHINGLES & SHAKES

Wood shingles and shakes are a manageable size and easy to handle. They require a backing that forms a fairly flat, sturdy nailing base. You can also put them over existing siding; they ride over slightly bumpy wall surfaces better than most siding materials do. Installation requires only standard carpentry tools. For more about tools, see page 52.

Exposure and coursing. Before applying shingles or shakes, you must determine the correct exposure for them (the amount of each shingle or shake to be exposed to the weather) and decide whether to use single or double courses (see drawings below).

SINGLE & DOUBLE COURSING

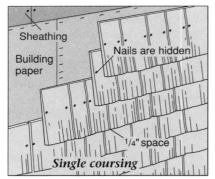

Sheathing
Building paper
Nails are hidden
1/4" space
Single coursing

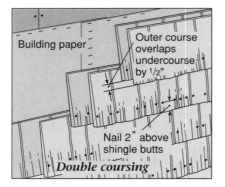

Building paper
Outer course overlaps undercourse by 1/2"
Nail 2" above shingle butts
Double coursing

Single coursing is more common, but double coursing creates deeper shadow lines and allows longer exposures and the use of lower-grade shingles as an undercourse. With standard double coursing, the nails are visible. Determine maximum exposure according to this chart.

MAXIMUM EXPOSURE

	Lengths	Single courses	Double courses
Shingles	16"	7½"	12"
	18"	8½"	14"
	24"	11½"	16"
Shakes	18"	8½"	14"
	24"	11½"	18"

Assuming that you've prepared the wall as described on page 96, measure the distance from the base chalk line to the soffit at both ends of the tallest wall. Compensate for any steps in the base chalk line and split any difference to figure the average distance from the soffit to the base line. Divide that distance by the maximum exposure for your shingles or shakes. If your computation doesn't yield a whole number of courses, decrease the exposure enough to make the courses come out evenly. Also adjust the number of courses to achieve a full exposure below windows.

As shown at right, make a story pole from a 1 by 2 the length of your tallest wall's height. Starting at one end, mark the story pole at intervals equal to the established exposure.

Holding or tacking the story pole flush with the base line, transfer the marks to each corner and to the trim at each window and door casing.

Note that if you plan to double-course, shingle or shake butts on the outer course should overlap the undercourse by ½ inch.

Nailing. Nails are concealed in single coursing, 1 inch above the line where the butts of the next higher course will go. For shingles, drive a nail ¾ inch in from each side (1 inch in for shakes) and then use additional nails every 4 inches between.

Use hot-dipped galvanized box or shingling nails, 1¼ inches or longer for shingles, 2 inches or longer for shakes. They should be long enough to penetrate sheathing or solid backing by at least 1 inch.

For double courses, place the nails 2 inches above the butt line, ¾ inch in from each edge, and at 4-inch intervals in between.

First courses. Nail on the first course of shingles, keeping the butts flush with the base chalk line (or ½ inch above it if you're double-coursing). You can use low-grade shingles for the first course whether you're single- or double-coursing—they will be covered by the next course. Allow expansion room between shingles or shakes: ¼ inch between shingles, ½ inch between shakes.

USING A STORY POLE

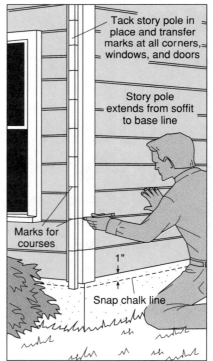

Tack story pole in place and transfer marks at all corners, windows, and doors

Story pole extends from soffit to base line

Marks for courses

1"

Snap chalk line

Directly over the first course, apply a second course. If you're double-coursing, overlap the original course by ½ inch. Offset all joints between shingles and shakes of different courses by at least 1½ inches so water will run off properly.

Successive courses. Lay successive courses from the first course to the soffit. As you finish each course, snap a chalk line over it or nail on a straight 1 by 4 board as a guide for laying the next course evenly.

If you double-course, use a shiplap board to align the butts of the undercourse and outer course.

Corners. Typical methods for finishing shingles at corners are shown below. For outside corners, bring shingles or shakes flush to a vertical 1 by 3 or 1 by 4. Or miter the corners—but prepare to spend a lot of time at it if you do. More typically, you can "weave" the corners by alternately overlapping them. Trim or plane the overlapping shingles flush.

At inside corners, bring shingles and shakes flush to a 1 by 1 or 2 by 2 nailed in the corner. Or miter or weave them, being sure to flash behind with right-angle metal flashing that extends 3 inches under the shingles or shakes of each wall.

Caulk the seams well at corners. Clear silicone looks better and lasts

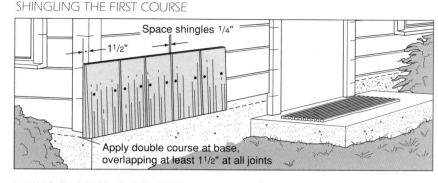

Space shingles ¼"

1½"

Apply double course at base, overlapping at least 1½" at all joints

LAYING SUCCESSIVE COURSES

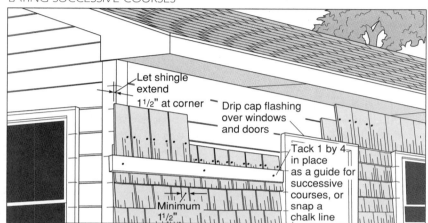

Let shingle extend 1½" at corner

Drip cap flashing over windows and doors

Tack 1 by 4 in place as a guide for successive courses, or snap a chalk line

Minimum 1½"

longer than latex caulk but will not take a stain or paint as well.

Obstacles. Shingles and shakes are easy to cut and fit around doors, windows, pipes, meters, and so forth. For curved cuts, use a coping saw or saber saw. Caulk well around edges.

Cornices. Cornices can be either open or closed. You can easily trim wood shingles or shakes to fit neatly around rafters in an open treatment. Closed cornices (see page 103) are best handled by installing tongue-and-groove or shiplap board siding finished to match the other trim.

TYPICAL CORNER TREATMENTS

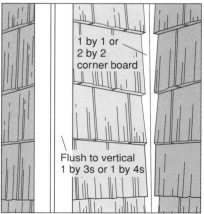

1 by 1 or 2 by 2 corner board

Flush to vertical 1 by 3s or 1 by 4s

Woven outside corner

Woven inside corner

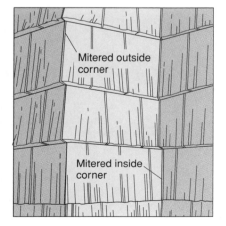

Mitered outside corner

Mitered inside corner

INSTALLING PLYWOOD & HARDBOARD PANEL SIDINGS

S iding panels of plywood and hardboard are popular because their large sizes (4 by 8, 9, or 10 feet) give quick coverage. In addition, plywood's strength can eliminate the need for bracing and sheathing on the wall's frame. Hardboard panels, nailed on according to the manufacturers' specifications, can also provide shear strength.

Codes determine the need for sheathing. As a rule, either material may be applied directly to studs on 16-inch centers without sheathing; some thick sizes of each material may be applied directly to studs on 24-inch centers. If you're putting panel siding over a nonstructural sheathing such as foam board, you must take special care to nail the siding material through the sheathing to framing.

Though codes may not demand the use of building paper or house wrap beneath plywood, it's a good idea to install this extra barrier under either plywood or hardboard sidings (see pages 97–98), particularly if the panel edges do not interlock or are not covered with battens. It's also important to brush all panel edges with a water sealant before installation.

Panels may be mounted either vertically or horizontally. Because vertical installation minimizes the number of horizontal joints, it's the preferred method. If you choose a horizontal pattern, stagger vertical end joints and nail the long, horizontal edges into fire blocks or other nailing supports.

Generally speaking, the main difference between using plywood and using hardboard is that, because hardboard is not as strong, it needs firmer backing and attachment.

Plywood and hardboard lap sidings are installed using methods similar to those used for installing board sidings. For more information, see page 101.

APPLYING PLYWOOD & HARDBOARD PANELS

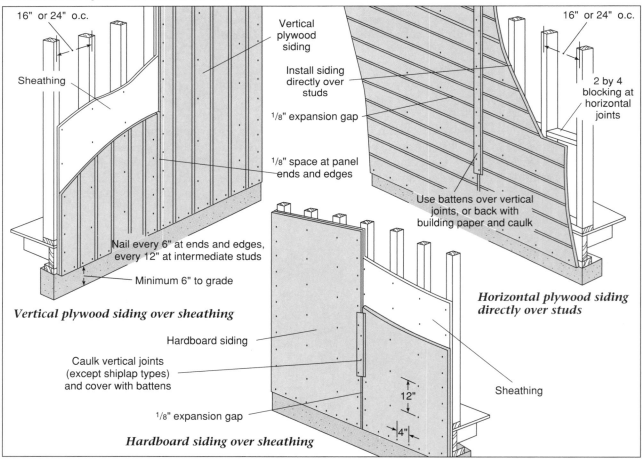

16" or 24" o.c.

Sheathing

Vertical plywood siding

Install siding directly over studs

1/8" expansion gap

1/8" space at panel ends and edges

Nail every 6" at ends and edges, every 12" at intermediate studs

Minimum 6" to grade

Vertical plywood siding over sheathing

16" or 24" o.c.

2 by 4 blocking at horizontal joints

Use battens over vertical joints, or back with building paper and caulk

Horizontal plywood siding directly over studs

Hardboard siding

Caulk vertical joints (except shiplap types) and cover with battens

1/8" expansion gap

12"

4"

Sheathing

Hardboard siding over sheathing

Nailing. You can nail either material with 6-penny or 8-penny corrosion-resistant common or box nails; the size depends upon the manufacturer's recommendations for application to your nailing base. For re-siding over wood boards or sheathing, use hot-dipped galvanized ring-shank nails. Don't use finishing nails, staples, T nails, or bugle-head nails. Hardboard manufacturers sell nails with heads colored to match factory finishes on the hardboard.

Nails should be long enough to penetrate studs or other backing by at least 1½ inches. For new siding nailed directly to studs, use 6-penny nails for ⅜-inch or ½-inch panels, 8-penny nails for ⅝-inch panels. Nail every 6 inches around the perimeter of each sheet and every 12 inches along studs or furring. If hardboard panels are meant to supply shear strength where not applied over sheathing, space nails every 4 inches around the perimeter and intermediately every 8 inches along studs.

When driving in nails, be careful not to "dimple" the panel's surface with the last hammer blow. Don't set nailheads below the surface.

When you nail a panel, first tack it in position with nails at each corner (leave these nailheads protruding so you can pull them if necessary). Then nail from top to bottom along one edge (the edge adjoining the preceding panel). Move to the next stud or furring strip and nail along it; move on to the next support; and so on. This method prevents the panel from buckling in the center.

The first step.
Before you begin putting up panels, you'll need to figure how long they should be; measure from the base chalk line to the soffit. If you plan to create a closed cornice (see page 113), it may be simpler to install the soffit before the siding panels.

Should the distance from base line to soffit be longer than the siding

Flush at eaves

Align edge with stud

Mark for cutting

Panel's edge

Back lap

Front lap

Overlap old siding by 1"

sheets, you'll need to join panels end to end, using one of the methods for horizontal joints shown on the facing page.

The first sheet.
To begin your installation, position the first sheet at an outside corner, its bottom edge flush with the base line. Check with a carpenter's level to make sure vertical edges are plumb. If the corner itself isn't plumb, you'll need to trim the panel edge to align with it. Hold or tack the sheet in place, flush with the base line, and trace along the outermost points of the existing siding or framing from top to bottom; the inside vertical edge must be centered over a stud, furring strip, or other firm backing.

Take the panel down and cut along the line you traced, using a circular saw or handsaw. Nail the trimmed panel in place.

Successive sheets.
The next sheet butts against the first sheet, often with an overlapping shiplap vertical edge (see detail in drawing on page 112). Leave a ¹⁄₁₆-inch expansion gap at all joints (in humid climates, leave ⅛ inch). Sheets must join over studs, blocking, or other sturdy backing. Be careful not to nail through both parts of the laps.

If your panel doesn't have a shiplap edge, caulk along the vertical edges and butt them loosely together, leaving about ¹⁄₁₆ inch for expansion. Unless there's building paper or house wrap behind each joint, you'll need to cover the joints with battens —1 by 2, 1 by 3, or 1 by 4 strips that protect seams.

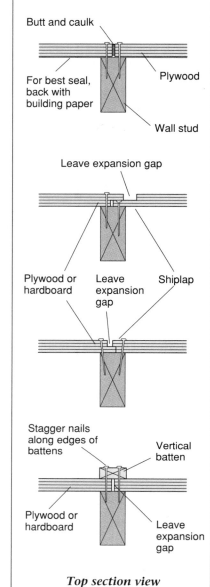

Top section view

Obstacles. As you install sheets, you may encounter some obstacles such as gas pipes or hose bibbs. Cut out a section with a saber saw so the sheet can be put in place (see detail in drawing above). Mount and nail the sheet; then fashion a cutout to fit around the protrusion and fasten that area in place with glue and—if possible—with nails.

Corners. Panel siding requires special corner construction to ensure a weatherproof joint. Outside corners can be rabbeted together and caulked or covered by 1 by 3 and 1 by 4 trim boards; inside corners are generally just caulked and butted together. You can also use a vertical corner trim board, such as a 2 by 2 (see drawings, on facing page, top left and center).

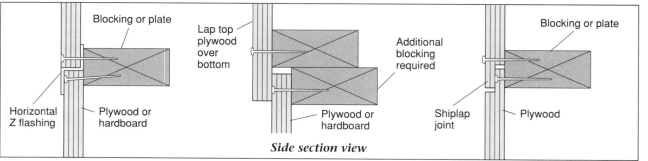

Side section view

INSIDE CORNERS

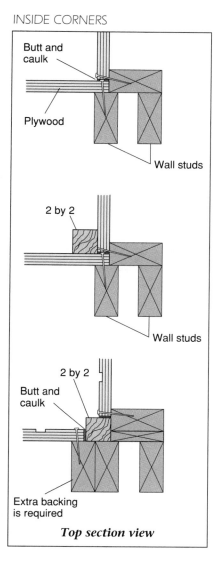

Butt and caulk

Plywood

Wall studs

2 by 2

Wall studs

2 by 2

Butt and caulk

Extra backing is required

Top section view

OUTSIDE CORNERS

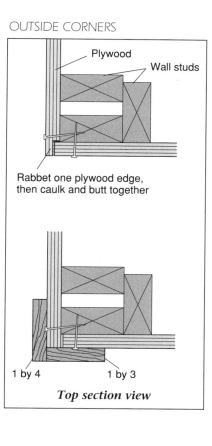

Plywood

Wall studs

Rabbet one plywood edge, then caulk and butt together

1 by 4   1 by 3

Top section view

CORNICES

Open cornice

Vent

Fit plywood around rafters

Closed cornice

2 by 2

Plowed fascia board

Soffit vents

Plywood

If the plywood panels are milled with grooves, the grooves under corner boards might let dirt and water penetrate. To prevent this, nail the vertical trim boards directly to the corner studs or existing siding, caulk along the edges, and butt the plywood against them.

Window and door openings.
When dealing with these large areas, remember the carpenter's maxim, "Measure twice, cut once." For ease of fitting, allow an extra ³⁄₁₆-inch gap around all openings. If possible, center the seams between sheets over or under the opening.

Use a carpenter's square or chalk line to lay out cuts, a circular saw for straight cutting, and a saber saw for cutting corners and curves. Since these saws cut on the upstroke, cut the sheets on the back side so you won't splinter the face. But don't forget, when laying out the lines, that the sheet will be flipped during installation. For straight cuts, you can make a guide as shown below.

CIRCULAR SAW GUIDE

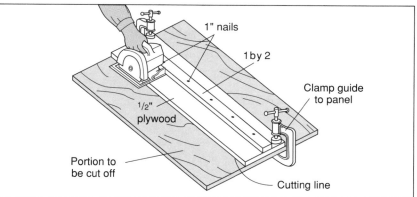

1" nails

1 by 2

Clamp guide to panel

½" plywood

Portion to be cut off

Cutting line

Cornices. On panel-sided houses, cornices are usually closed—an open cornice requires very precisely made cuts to fit snugly around rafters. Consider running a plowed fascia board along rafter tails and a 2-by-2 block along the wall, and attaching lengths of siding along the soffit, as detailed in the drawings above.

SIDING REPAIRS & MAINTENANCE

 ll it takes is a small break in your house's siding to start early deterioration. Rain will run down the wall and find this opening, seeping behind paint and into the wall's interior. Then paint will blister and peel, more water will penetrate the wall, and the problem will escalate. Before you know it, you've got structural damage inside the wall.

Paying attention to problems promptly can spare you much larger repairs later.

Put in a few hours of preventive maintenance every spring and fall. Clean your siding to keep it looking fresh, watch for any chipped or peeling areas, and keep all joints and seams sealed with caulking compound (see page 85).

Even well-maintained siding may be damaged by an errant baseball, a wayward lawnmower, or a careless driver. Fortunately, most siding problems are quite limited and can be handled with relative ease—though some may call for the talents of a contractor.

In this chapter, you'll find techniques for repairs you can do yourself. With proper care and maintenance, all siding materials should give many years of service.

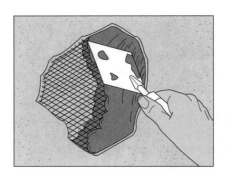

REPAIRING WOOD SIDINGS

amage to wood siding materials can usually be repaired fairly easily.

MINOR SPOT REPAIRS

Most repairs involve filling holes, fixing split or warped boards, and/or repainting. Siding that's badly damaged should be replaced.

Repairing holes. Small holes can be filled with wood putty or a flexible, all-purpose filler sometimes sold as "premixed bridging and patching compound." Putty comes in shades that match stained wood; the filler, which does a better job of accommodating the wood's expansion and contraction, is meant to be painted and sanded after application. Caulking compound can be used for some deep holes but cannot be sanded.

To conceal a small hole, fill it, and allow the filler to dry. If the hole is fairly large, apply several layers, letting each one dry completely before you add the next. When the final layer is dry, sand it smooth, then finish the patch to match the siding.

Repairing split boards. A clean split or crack can be repaired by prying the board apart and coating both edges with waterproof glue, as shown at right. Then either nail or screw the board back into position or, for a less visible repair, drive a row of temporary nails just under the lower edge of the board and bend them up over the edge to hold the board in place. Remove the nails after the glue has set. Fill the crack with putty or a flexible filler, as described above.

Repairing warped boards. If boards have been fitted too close together during installation, they may warp or buckle when moisture makes them swell.

To straighten such a board, first try to pull it into line by driving long screws through it and into the wall studs (use a portable electric drill to make pilot holes for the screws). Cover the screw holes with wood putty or flexible filler; then sand and finish as you would after repairing holes in siding.

If that doesn't work, you'll have to trim the affected board to give it more room. Pull out the nails within the warped area or cut them with a hacksaw blade. Continue removing nails to the nearest end of the board. Pull the end of the board outward; then file it with a rasp, sand it with sandpaper, or shave the end a little at a time with a block plane until the board fits. Renail the board.

Fixing paint problems. Paint problems can result from a number of causes: use of the wrong kind of paint, improper surface preparation before painting, careless painting, exposure to harsh sunlight over a long period of time, inadequate wall ventilation. For advice about dealing with paint problems, see page 123.

SQUARING UP THE ENDS

Block plane

REPLACING BOARDS

Sometimes a board can be so badly damaged or decayed that your only choice is to replace it. How you go about this depends on how the boards were milled and how they were nailed. The trickiest part of the job may be finding wood that matches the original.

No matter what type of siding you're replacing, you'll have to cut the damaged piece and remove the nails in order to pry it out. Wherever possible, center your cuts over wall studs. For best results, cut out and replace a section that spans at least three studs, making cutting lines with a carpenter's square to keep cuts at right angles. Remove nails from the

HOW TO MEND A SPLIT BOARD

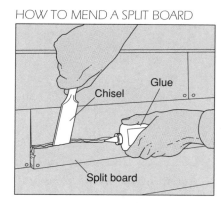

Chisel — Glue

Split board

1) Carefully pry the damaged board apart at the crack and coat the edges of both pieces with waterproof glue.

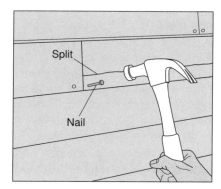

Split

Nail

2) Push glued edges together tightly and secure both sections to the sheathing with nails or screws through predrilled holes.

COMMON BOARD SIDINGS

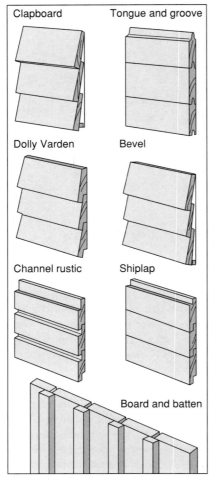

Clapboard Tongue and groove

Dolly Varden Bevel

Channel rustic Shiplap

Board and batten

old siding with a prybar or nail puller, or cut off nailheads with a hacksaw blade. Use plastic roofing cement to seal any tears in the building paper. Then carefully measure and cut the new piece.

Tongue-and-groove siding. Because the boards are locked together by the tongues and grooves, the damaged piece must be split lengthwise as well as cut at the ends, as shown at right, before it can be removed.

It's easiest to make the cuts with a circular saw. Set the blade depth just shy of the thickness of the siding and saw almost to each edge, holding the blade guard back and dipping the moving blade down into the wood to

start each cut. Hold the saw firmly—it may kick back—and be careful not to cut into adjacent boards.

Overlapping sidings. Clapboard, bevel, Dolly Varden, shiplap, channel rustic, and other overlapping styles are face-nailed to studs or sheathing. Though the boards overlap, you can replace a damaged piece without removing other boards (you may need to pry up the board above the piece you're replacing to free the last bits of damaged board). To replace any overlapping siding, follow the directions for replacing clapboard siding, illustrated on the facing page.

To provide a solid nailing base for the replacement board, center the end cuts over studs, wherever possible. You can use a backsaw to cut clapboard, bevel, or Dolly Varden siding; cut shiplap or channel rustic siding with a circular saw. If nails are in the way of your saw cuts, pull them out and replace them later.

Board-and-batten siding. To remove board-and-batten siding, pry up the battens on either side of the damaged board far enough to raise the nailheads, then pull out the nails. Repeat this process until you're able to remove the damaged board.

HOW TO REPLACE TONGUE-AND-GROOVE SIDING

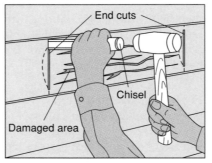

1) Pull out all exposed nails in the area to be removed. Mark lines for end cuts, then use a circular saw to cut almost to the top and bottom of each mark. Finish the cuts with a mallet and chisel.

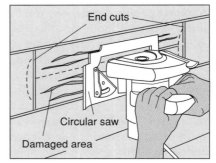

2) Rip along the center of the damaged section with the circular saw, cutting almost to the end cuts. Again, complete the cuts at both ends with a mallet and chisel or handsaw.

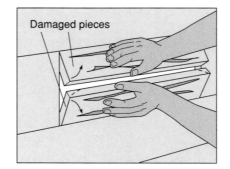

3) Carefully cave in the damaged board; then pull out all of the loosened pieces. If you find any cuts or tears in the building paper, repair them with some plastic roofing cement.

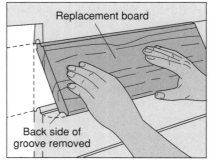

4) Remove the back side of the groove on the replacement board and slide it in place; face-nail the board. Countersink nailheads, use flexible filler on board ends and nail holes, then finish surface.

Patch any cuts or tears that you find in the building paper with plastic roofing cement. Replace the damaged board and battens with new ones cut to match. Seal all joints with flexible filler. Then sand and either stain or paint to blend with the existing siding.

REPLACING SHINGLES & SHAKES

When a shingle or shake splits, curls, warps, or breaks, you may be able to nail down the cracked or warped pieces and cover the nailheads with silicone caulking compound. Otherwise, you must replace the entire shingle or shake—a quick and easy job. The replacement technique depends on whether the shingles or shakes are in single or double courses (see page 108).

In a single-course installation, each course overlaps the one below by at least half the length of a shingle or shake. The nails in each course are concealed by the course above. Replacement procedures are the same as for a shingle or shake roof (see page 91).

Double coursing employs two complete layers of shingles or shakes with the nailheads exposed. To replace a damaged shingle or shake, simply pull out the nails, remove the damaged piece, slide in a replacement that's the same size, and nail it with rust-resistant nails.

To blend the color of new cedar shingles with the grayish tones of aged cedar, you can use a bleaching oil or stain (see page 122) or, for just a few shingles, try a solution of 1½ pounds of baking soda and a dash of dish detergent to a gallon of warm water. Paint this on, let it set, rinse, and repeat. This solution causes a chemical reaction that approximates the look of natural weathering.

HOW TO REPLACE CLAPBOARD SIDING

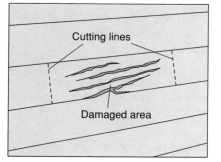

1) Mark cutting lines on each side of the damaged area, centering the lines over the wall studs. (If the damage is near a joint in the siding, you'll need to make only one cut.)

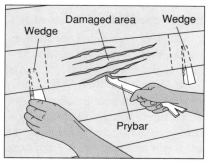

2) Lift the bottom edge of the damaged board with a prybar or stout chisel. Drive small wedges underneath the board outside both cutting lines to keep it raised.

3) With a handsaw or backsaw, cut through the board along both cutting lines; finish the cuts with a keyhole saw or a chisel. Break the damaged board out—in pieces, if necessary.

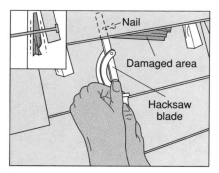

4) Cut any nails passing through the board above with a hacksaw blade or pull them out to free the top of the damaged board. Repair any tears in the building paper with roofing cement.

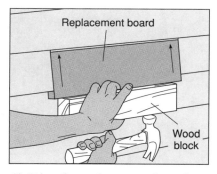

5) Trim the replacement board to the right length (measure across both top and bottom) and drive it into the exact position, hammering upward against a wood block placed along its lower edge.

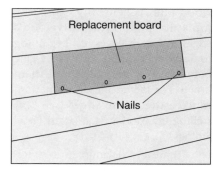

6) Nail down the replacement board in the same way the surrounding siding was attached. Fill the nail holes and board ends with flexible filler, then stain or paint the new board.

REPAIRING PLYWOOD & HARDBOARD SIDINGS

Because of both their makeup and their size, plywood and hardboard panel sidings are repaired differently than wood board sidings. Damaged lap panels are replaced the same way as solid wood sidings (see page 115).

REPAIRING PLYWOOD SIDING

The most common repair jobs involving plywood are fixing areas where the surface is "checking" (showing small splits), regluing layers that are delaminating (separating), and, with more extensive problems, replacing damaged sections.

Checking. Surface veneers are thin and so have a tendency to split and peel when left to weather unprotected. Sand down checks and fill with wood putty or a flexible, all-purpose filler (see page 115). Sand again, then refinish to match existing siding.

Delamination. The separation of wood plies is generally caused by moisture penetrating plywood's edges. To repair edges just beginning to delaminate, apply waterproof glue between plies and then nail them down. For large-scale delamination, replace the entire sheet (see "Installing Plywood & Hardboard Panel Sidings," pages 110–113).

To prevent delamination, waterproof the edges with a sealant during installation, use proper flashing at joints, apply caulking compound where materials meet (see page 85), and maintain stained or painted finishes in a timely way.

Damaged plywood. Don't try to repair broken or badly damaged plywood; replace it. You can replace part of a sheet, but it's neater and easier to replace the entire sheet; otherwise, you'll have to put 2-by-4 backing around the edges of the replacement piece (unless the siding is already backed by sheathing).

To remove plywood, pull off any battens covering joints or used as trim. Wedge a chisel into the joints and pry the edges of the damaged panel enough to lift the nailheads and pull the nails. Remove the sheet and repair any damage to the underlayment or building paper, using plastic roofing cement.

Mount and nail on the replacement sheet (see pages, 110–113). Caulk the joints, replace battens or trim, and finish the surface to match.

To remove a damaged section, use a circular saw. Mark cuts with a square, and center vertical cuts over studs. Use a handsaw at the corners.

Use 2-by-4 backing where needed to support edges of the replacement piece. Cut the replacement to fit, repair any tears in the building paper with plastic roofing cement, and nail the new piece in place. Caulk seams and finish to match.

REPAIRING HARDBOARD SIDING

With hardboard siding, you may see small holes, buckling, stains, or damaged areas. Here's how to fix them.

Small holes. Fill any small holes in hardboard with flexible, all-purpose filler; then sand and paint. If a hole is fairly deep, build the patch up gradually, filling two or three times before the final sanding.

Buckling. This can be caused by improper nailing or by moisture. Check the nailing first. If the siding isn't fastened with properly spaced box nails that are long enough to penetrate studs at least 1½ inches (see page 110), renail correctly.

If outside moisture hasn't been repelled by the finish, this may be the culprit (see page 123).

Stains. Stains can usually be removed with mild detergent or—for oil-based stains—a solvent.

Major damage. If panels are badly damaged, remove them and replace them with new ones, following the instructions for plywood.

REPAIRING DAMAGED PANELS

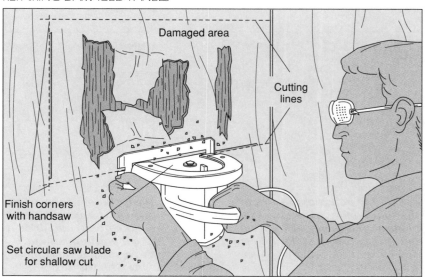

Damaged area

Cutting lines

Finish corners with handsaw

Set circular saw blade for shallow cut

REPAIRING ALUMINUM & VINYL SIDINGS

Both aluminum and vinyl siding panels have interlocking flanges along their edges. Each panel is nailed to the sheathing through slots along one flange; the other flange interlocks with the adjacent panel. Some panels are meant to be installed vertically, others horizontally.

You can successfully repair minor dents, scratches, and corrosion in aluminum siding. Vinyl siding and extensively damaged aluminum siding must usually be replaced.

REPAIRING ALUMINUM SIDING

To remove a dent in aluminum siding, drill a hole in the center of the dent and screw in a self-tapping screw with two washers under the screw head (the screw cuts its own thread as it's driven in). Gently pull on the screw head with a pair of pliers. Remove the screw and fill the hole with plastic aluminum filler (follow directions on the tube). When dry, sand the filler smooth and touch up with matching paint.

Conceal scratches in aluminum siding by applying metal primer. When the primer is dry, coat with acrylic latex house paint to match.

Clean off any corrosion with fine steel wool, prime the area with metal primer, and cover with latex paint, following label directions.

REPLACING ALUMINUM SIDING

If a section of your aluminum siding is damaged beyond a simple surface repair, you can replace it. Be advised, though, that many of the manufacturers who made metal siding in the '50s and '60s are no longer in business, so currently available materials may not match yours. If this is the case, borrow a piece from an inconspicuous part of your house or garage—replacing it with a similar material.

You start by cutting out the damaged part of the panel, using a utility knife to score it several times so you can bend it back and forth to break it off. Leave the upper, nailed portion in place. Use tin snips to cut the new replacement section of siding long enough to overlap the existing siding by 3 inches on each side. Apply butyl gutter seal along the existing nailing strip and press the replacement piece into place, hooking the base into the interlocking edge of the section below. Hold or prop until dry.

REPLACING VINYL SIDING

If vinyl siding is cracked or punctured, remove the entire damaged section before installing a replacement piece. To separate interlocking panels, you'll need a special tool called a "zip tool" or "unlocking tool." It's best to do the work during warm weather, when the vinyl is pliable.

With the zip tool, unlock the panel adjacent to or above the damaged one and lift it up to expose the nails securing the damaged panel. Bend out the adjacent panel carefully and remove the nails holding the damaged one. Using a pencil and a carpenter's square, mark cutting lines on each side of the damaged area. With tin snips or a backsaw, cut the panel along the lines and remove the damaged section.

Cut a replacement piece 2 inches longer than the section removed to allow for a 1-inch overlap at each end. (Cut only 1 inch longer if the damaged section ends at a corner or joint.) Snap the top edge of the new section in place and nail it with aluminum or galvanized box nails long enough to penetrate at least 1 inch into the sheathing. Using the zip tool, hook the upper panel over the new panel's lock.

HOW TO REPLACE ALUMINUM SIDING

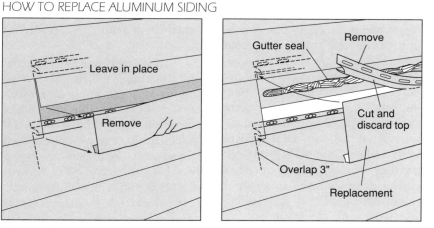

1) Cut through the center of the panel to just beyond both sides of the damaged area, using a utility knife. Make vertical cuts at both ends; remove the lower part of the damaged section, leaving the rest of the panel in place.

2) Cut the nailing strip off the replacement by scoring it with a utility knife and snapping it off. Generously apply butyl gutter seal to the remaining portion of damaged panel. Overlap each end by 3 inches.

REPAIRING STUCCO SIDING

Stucco walls typically consist of three layers of stucco applied over wire mesh. The final coat is either pigmented or painted and can be textured in a variety of ways. Because stucco is a rigid material, it cracks if a house moves with settling or earthquakes. It's also susceptible to moisture damage if it isn't applied properly.

Most important to a successful repair job are slow curing of the stucco and careful matching of color and texture to the existing wall.

Whether or not to repair your own stucco is a tough call. The chances are good that you can handle minor repairs successfully. But if problem areas are fairly extensive, it may be wise to have a professional do the work.

Cracks. You can fill and cover hairline and slightly larger cracks with a flexible, all-purpose filler. Or, if the patch won't need to be sanded, you can use caulking compound. If cracks are fairly deep, build up the patch with more than one layer of filler, allowing the filler to dry thoroughly between coats. Finish to match the existing walls.

To fix larger cracks, use a cold chisel and ball-peen hammer to undercut the edges of the crack in an inverted V (wear eye protection). Then brush away loose stucco, dust with a stiff brush, and dampen the crack with a fine spray of water.

With a mason's trowel or putty knife, fill the crack with stucco patching compound (available at home-improvement centers), packing it in tightly; texture to match the sur-

1) Remove loose material with a cold chisel and ball-peen hammer and replace wire mesh as needed.

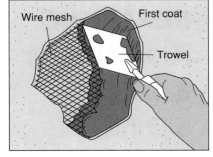

2) Wet hole, then apply base coat to within ½ inch of surface. Scratch surface.

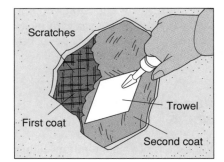

3) Dampen first coat. Apply second coat to within ⅛ inch of surface. Let dry.

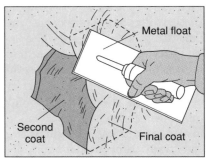

4) Dampen area, apply final coat, and texture to match existing wall. Allow to cure four days.

rounding stucco. Cure the stucco patch by dampening it once or twice a day for about four days.

Small holes. To repair a small hole (up to about 6 inches in diameter), first remove loose stucco with a cold chisel and ball-peen hammer, undercutting the edges, and blow out any dust. Be careful not to damage building paper. If the wire mesh is damaged, staple in a new piece. Dampen the patching site with a fine spray of water and pack the hole with stucco patching compound, using a mason's trowel or putty knife to apply it smoothly. To cure the new stucco, keep it damp for about four days.

Large holes. For larger holes, you'll need to apply three coats of stucco, as with a new wall. The first and second coats are made from 1 part Portland cement, 3 parts coarse sand, and

⅒ part hydrated lime, with enough water to make a fairly stiff paste. For the final coat, use 1 part Portland cement, 3 parts coarse sand, and ¼ part hydrated lime (use white Portland cement and sand if you're adding pigment to the stucco).

Start by removing loose material and replacing any damaged or missing mesh. Next, apply a "scratch coat" to within ½ inch of the surface. Scratch this fairly stiff coat with a nail so subsequent coats will adhere. Keep it damp with a light spray of water for two days, then apply the "brown coat" to within ⅛ inch of the surface. Let this coat cure, keeping it damp for another two days. Finally, dampen the area and apply the top coat, texturing it to match the wall (and adding pigment if necessary). Allow this to dry slowly, moistening it with a fine spray for four days. If you plan to paint it, wait a month.

REPAIRING BRICK & STONE VENEER

Brick and stone veneers are usually applied over building paper to a wood-frame wall; the mortared joints may be tooled, or finished, in a number of ways. Properly tooled joints are essential to strong, watertight walls.

Most problems with brick or stone veneer develop at the mortar joints. The mortar can shrink, causing the joints to open. Old-fashioned lime-base mortar can crumble. And freeze-thaw cycles in cold-winter climates, excess moisture, and settling can also break down the mortar.

To repair cracked or crumbling mortar, you'll have to remove the old mortar and repoint the joints (fill them with new mortar).

Though you can make your own mortar, it's easier to use dry ready-mixed mortar (use weather-resistant type N), available at building supply stores; follow package directions. When filling the joints, you may want to use a special tool called a "hawk" (see step 2 below) to hold the mortar conveniently close to the job.

Using a jointer, steel rod, or trowel, tool the new joints to match the existing ones. Mortar joints should be tooled when they are neither so soft that they smear the wall nor so hard that a metal tool leaves marks. Keep tooled joints damp for about four days while the mortar cures.

CAUTION: When chipping out old mortar with a mallet or ball-peen hammer and cold chisel, protect your eyes by wearing goggles.

HOW TO REPOINT DAMAGED MORTAR JOINTS

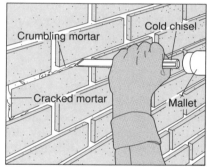

1) Wearing goggles, chip out cracked mortar to a depth of at least ½ inch, using a cold chisel and mallet. Clean the joints with a wire brush and dampen them.

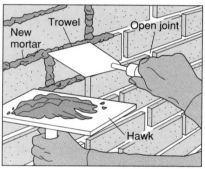

2) Pack mortar into open and dampened (not wet) joints, using a small trowel and a hawk. Tamp the mortar with a trowel or with a piece of wood.

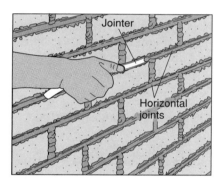

3) When mortar has set to the right consistency, finish the horizontal (bed) joints by pressing and drawing a jointer (or rod or trowel) along each one.

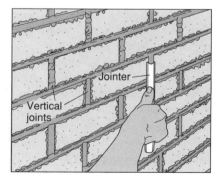

4) Finish the vertical (head) joints in the same manner as the horizontal ones, pressing and drawing the tool along each joint to match the existing ones.

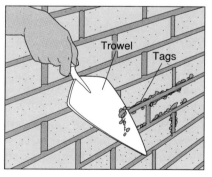

5) Cut off any tags (excess mortar) by sliding the trowel along the wall. Finish the horizontal and vertical joints again (see steps 3 and 4).

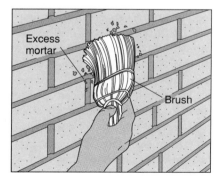

6) When mortar is well set, brush the wall with a stiff brush or broom. Keep the joints damp for about four days so mortar can fully cure.

FINISHING YOUR SIDING

With wood and metal sidings, a proper finish is the first line of defense against the elements. If the siding's finish is blistering or cracked and peeling, a house not only looks shabby but is vulnerable to moisture problems and other types of weather damage.

Some sidings need to be finished, and some don't. Each material has its own finishing requirements—or lack of them. The same material type may have several possibilities. Some plywood sidings, for example, come prefinished; some are primed; still others are finished once in place.

Here are some of the basics.

FINISHES FOR WOOD SIDING

Several different finishes are used to protect natural wood siding, making it possible to attain just about any appearance. Of course, a finish does much more than create a look—it protects wood from the damaging effects of water, sunlight, mildew, and general wear.

Though you may like the natural look of unfinished cedar, it's important to apply some type of finish to protect wood against cupping and splitting, mold, ultraviolet degradation—even smog and dirt. By choosing the right finish, you can get the look of weathered wood (or any other appearance) with years of durability.

Do not use lacquers, varnishes, or other clear finishes that form a film. These are vulnerable to sunlight damage and may become brittle and crack and peel. Also avoid linseed oil or turpentine mixtures, which attract dirt and mildew.

Wood siding finishes can be divided into four categories: clear water repellents, bleaching oils and stains, pigmented stains, and paints and primers.

Clear water repellents. This is the least protective type of finish for siding, though it's best at retaining the natural look of wood. As the name implies, clear repellents do not add color or hide the wood grain but do repel moisture to protect wood from moisture-related weathering. Though they offer only minimal protection against the sun's deterioration of wood fibers, some types contain ultraviolet blocks that reduce the sun's effects. To fortify their protection, some types contain a mildewcide and/or a preservative.

These finishes offer protection from six months to two years.

Bleaching oils and bleaching stains. These products, sometimes referred to as "weathering stains," create a weathered look quickly and offer more protection than water repellents. Used primarily with cedar siding, they color wood gray when applied, then work with sun and moisture to create an even, weathered look over a period of six months to a year. Because the protection they offer, used alone, lasts only two to three years, it's smart to apply a water repellent over the top every couple of years.

Stains. Stains are like thin paint; they are protective finishes that are pigmented to color wood. Any stain used for siding should contain a mildewcide and a water repellent.

Depending on the amount of pigment they contain, stains are classified as either semitransparent or opaque. Semitransparent stains reveal more of the wood's grain and texture; opaque stains produce a more uniform color, preserving an appearance of texture but obscuring wood grain.

Both types are made in both oil/alkyd- and water-base formulations. Though water-base stains don't penetrate quite as well as oil/alkyd-base stains, they accommodate changes in moisture and heat better. Though semitransparent stains do not form a surface film (they penetrate into the wood), some opaque stains do—making them more vulnerable to blistering and peeling and other problems.

As a rule, stains work best on rough or saw-textured wood surfaces. On smooth surfaces, semitransparent stains wear off more quickly and opaque stains are more likely to flake and blister.

Paints and primers. If the appropriate type of paint is properly applied, it offers the most protective, long-lasting finish for wood. And paint comes in an almost unlimited range of colors.

On new wood, you should apply a primer before painting. A primer offers strong adhesion to wood and bonds with the top coat. Some painters recommend tinting the primer toward the finish color to make top coat's coverage a little better.

Opinions differ on whether water-base acrylic latex primers or oil/alkyd-base primers are preferable. Oil/alkyd-base primers absorb into wood better and are more effective at blocking stains that tend to bleed through some woods such as Western red cedar (though you can buy latex stain-blocking primers). On the other hand, air quality laws in many states have greatly restricted the use of solvent-base primers and paints.

You can put either a water-base or oil/alkyd-base top coat over an oil/alkyd-base primer or paint, but you shouldn't put an oil/alkyd-base top coat over a water-base primer or paint.

For the top coat, acrylic latex paints are generally the best choice because they are more flexible and "breathe" (allow water vapor to travel through wood). They're also easier to use because they clean up with water. Oil/alkyd-base paints dry harder but trap moisture and don't give with changes in heat and humidity, so they're more likely to peel or blister than latex paints.

One of the best ways to treat the surface of new wood siding is to apply a base coat of water repellent, an oil/alkyd-base primer, and one top coat of high-quality acrylic-latex paint. With high-quality paints, two top coats are not usually needed, especially if you tint the primer toward the finish color; but two top coats would, of course, provide even greater durability.

FINISHES FOR OTHER SIDINGS

Shingles, shakes, and plywood sidings can be protected with the same finishes as those used for wood board siding. Hardboard, vinyl, and metal may call for different finishing methods or materials.

Shingles and shakes. Most shingles and shakes are made of cedar, which is naturally resistant to decay. If you like the natural, rustic look of weathered shingles, you can leave them unfinished.

But if you want to control the appearance more, you must consider stains or paints. Of the two, exterior stain is usually the better choice because it doesn't form the same type of surface film as paint. A surface film can trap moisture in wood, eventually blistering and peeling. When this happens, it's difficult to scrape the

Exterior Paint Problems on Wood

Damage to painted wood surfaces can result from any of a number of causes. Before you repaint, try to analyze the cause so the problem won't come up again and your repair will be lasting.

Typical causes of paint damage include improper surface preparation, careless painting, use of the wrong paint, and structural problems that trap moisture in the wood. Common paint problems and their causes are described below.

■ *Blistering.* Paint blisters when water or solvent vapor is trapped underneath it. Cut the blister open. If you find bare wood underneath, the blister was created by moisture escaping from damp wood. If you find paint underneath, the solvent has blistered, possibly because of painting in direct sunlight or on wet wood.

■ *Peeling.* Paint peels and curls away from wood when it's applied over dirty, greasy, or wet wood or over loose paint.

■ *Alligatoring.* A checkered pattern of cracks resembling alligator skin results when the top coat is applied before the bottom coat is dry or when the paints in the bottom and top coats are incompatible.

■ *Wrinkling.* Wrinkles are caused by careless painting. If paint is applied too thickly, the top surface dries too rapidly and the paint underneath droops down.

■ *Chalking.* High-quality exterior paint is designed to chalk so rain will clean dirt from the surface. But chalking that comes off when you rub up against the surface indicates that the surface was unprimed or finished with paint of poor quality.

BLISTERING

PEELING

ALLIGATORING

WRINKLING

rough surfaces of shingles or shakes in preparation for a new coat of paint.

Both transparent and opaque water-base stains may be applied to shingles and shakes. Once you apply pigmented stain, though, plan to re-treat your siding every few years.

If you decide to paint shingles or shakes, use a stain-blocking latex primer before applying an acrylic latex paint.

In warm, humid climates, where fungus can attack wood, it's smart to apply a clear wood preservative containing a fungicide and a mildew retardant, available at paint stores.

Plywood. Because this is a wood product, the same types of finishes are used as for wood board siding (see page 122). Top grades of textured plywood can be finished with semitransparent oil/alkyd-base stain to preserve both the grain and the texture of the wood.

Most homeowners stain other grades of textured plywood with a heavier-bodied, water-base opaque stain that obscures the differences in color between the original surface and repair patches.

Paint can also be used over textured plywood and is the only finish recommended for sanded plywood or plywood overlaid with resin.

Because some woods, especially redwood, have natural stains that can bleed through latex paint, first apply an oil/alkyd-base primer or a specially formulated stain-blocking acrylic latex primer. For the top coat, use a high-quality acrylic latex paint.

Hardboard. Hardboard siding is sold factory finished, factory primed, or unfinished. Factory finishes are extremely durable—often backed by 15-year (or longer) warranties. For these prefinished types, you can get color-matched caulking compound, touch-up paint, and nails (except for some systems designed for hidden-nail application).

Primed hardboard siding is ready to paint with one or two top coats. Acrylic latex paint is the recommended choice. If the hardboard isn't primed, first apply a coat of oil/alkyd primer.

Vinyl siding. Vinyl siding doesn't require a finish. Its color goes right through the material, so scratches don't show. Maintain vinyl panels by simply hosing and sponging with a mild liquid detergent every few months.

If you want to change the color of existing vinyl siding, you may have a problem. The ability of vinyl to receive and hold paint satisfactorily is debatable. Check with the manufacturer of your vinyl siding for recommendations on painting.

Aluminum and steel. Factory-finished aluminum and steel sidings have a coating superior to anything a homeowner can apply. Usually, the factory finish—a baked-on enamel or an acrylic or vinyl overlay—is guaranteed for at least five years.

Of course, if your metal siding has seen better days or you want to change the color, painting is the easiest answer. Choose a high-quality acrylic paint. Before you paint, wash the siding with warm, soapy water and a scouring pad to remove chalk buildup. Then seal any seams with silicone caulking compound and spot-prime any areas where metal is exposed, using a good metal primer.

PAINTING TECHNIQUES

Painting is a task most homeowners can accomplish if the house isn't too tall or too large or too steeply situated. The evolution of painting into a fairly easy do-it-yourself job began with the introduction of the paint roller and easy-to-apply paints. Now, thanks to a variety of painting aids that range from electric heat guns to

paint sprayers, the task is easier than ever.

If you plan to paint your siding, here are some helpful tips.

Preparing the surface. Surface preparation makes a successful paint job. Start by repairing any damaged areas, as discussed in the chapter that begins on page 114. Then clean the siding. Surfaces must be clean, dry, and in good condition before you repaint.

On exterior wood surfaces, it is essential to remove old paint if it is peeling, blistering, or flaking. Sanding (best on smooth wood surfaces) and scraping (easy but time-consuming) are the techniques best suited to the home craftsperson. A wire brush works well on metal, masonry, and some wood surfaces.

There are two tools that can make paint removal easier—the power washer and the heat gun. Both can be rented. A power washer blasts a powerful spray of water, removing dirt and flaking paint and reducing the amount of scraping you'll need to do. A heat gun, which blows out hot air like a high-powered hair dryer, helps remove stubborn paint.

On stucco, steel, and masonry sidings, an alternative method (although expensive, messy, and very loud) is sandblasting, which can remove a tremendous amount of material very quickly. You can rent the equipment, but you're better off hiring professionals for this kind of job.

After scraping or stripping your house, wash it with a mild detergent, then hose it off. Allow the house to dry thoroughly. Caulk any seams or openings with a paintable caulking compound.

On steel, a chemical rust retardant should be applied either before painting or in combination with the paint. If you have a painted masonry surface that is only slightly chalked, it can be covered with a sealer and then repainted.

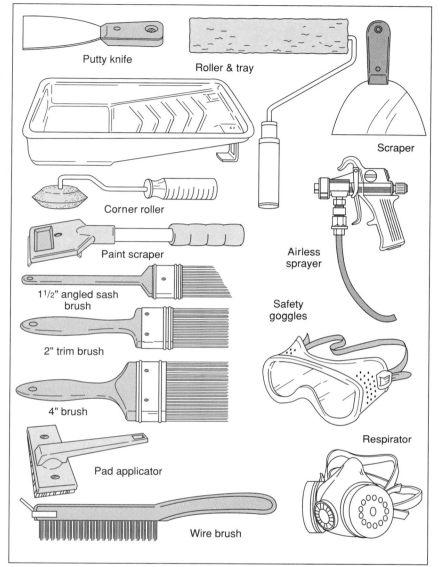

Putty knife

Roller & tray

Scraper

Corner roller

Paint scraper

Airless
sprayer

1¹/²" angled sash
brush

Safety
goggles

2" trim brush

4" brush

Respirator

Pad applicator

Wire brush

you intend to spray, follow the paint manufacturer's directions. In most cases, it takes two coats to get full coverage. And, to ensure good adhesion, it's usually best to brush or roll on the primer even if you intend to spray the top coats.

Using an airless sprayer will minimize overspray. With this tool, air pressure directed into a holding tank forces paint into a single hose leading to the spray nozzle. When you pull a trigger, the paint is forced out under pressure and atomized by the nozzle into a wide cone. Since the paint is not mixed with air, it drifts very little.

An airless spray gun can be very dangerous if handled improperly. At close range, the nozzle pressure is high enough to inject paint under the painter's skin. If you rent an airless sprayer, be sure to follow the instructions meticulously and wear protective goggles and a respirator-type paint mask.

Painting tips. Exterior painting is best done during fair, dry weather when the temperature is between 50° and 90°F. Wait until the morning dew has evaporated, and stop painting before evening dampness sets in. Avoid painting during windy or dusty weather, particularly if you're using slow-drying solvent-base finishes. (If insects get caught in wet paint, brush them off after it dries.)

Remove shutters and screens and paint them on a flat surface first. Paint windows, trim, and doors next. Paint the walls last so you won't have to lean a ladder against newly painted surfaces to do the windows and trim. Start at the top and work down, painting in the direction of the grain (if you're painting wood or wood lookalikes).

Last, be sure to follow the label directions for the finish. A careful job combined with close adherence to recommendations will make your finishing touches both beautiful and durable enough to last for years.

Gathering painting equipment.
Once you've chosen the proper paint or finish for your siding, it's time to gather the necessary tools and equipment. Both in preparing the siding and in painting it, plan to use plastic or cotton drop cloths to protect any fences, decks, patios, or shrubs near the house.

Though brushing on paint usually yields the best results, you can also use a roller, pad, or spray—depending upon the surface you're painting. Various tools are shown above.

Be sure to get a high-quality 2-inch trim brush and a 4-inch brush for painting wide surfaces. If your siding material has large, flat areas, you can paint with a 9-inch roller. Get a roller with a fine nap for smooth surfaces; a thicker nap is better for heavily textured surfaces. Buy an 8-foot extension for the roller so you can reach high areas.

Or rent a sprayer. Spray painting is the fastest way to cover a rough-textured surface such as shingles, stucco, or board-and-batten siding. If

INFORMATION SOURCES

MANUFACTURERS

ABTco, Inc.
3250 W. Big Beaver Road
Troy, MI 48084
(800) 521-4250
(Architectural trim)
and
Box 98
Highway 268
Roaring River, NC 28669
(800) 334-3551
(919) 696-2751
(Wood-based siding)

AEP Span
5100 E. Grand Avenue
Dallas, TX 75223
(800) 527-2503
(Metal roofing)

Alcan Building Products
11 Cragwood Road
Woodbridge, NJ 07095
(800) 729-2522
(Aluminum and vinyl siding)

Alcoa Building Products
Box 716
Sidney, OH 45365
(800) 621-7466
(Metal roofing; metal and vinyl siding)

Anthony Forest Products Co.
Box 1877
El Dorado, AR 71730
(800) 221-2326
(Wood-based siding)

ASC Pacific, Inc.
2110 Enterprise Boulevard
West Sacramento, CA 95691
(800) 726-2727
(Metal roofing)

ATAS Aluminum Corp.
6612 Snowdrift Road
Allentown, PA 18106
(800) 468-1441
(215) 395-8445
(Metal roofing and siding)

Awnair
43–57 Harrison Avenue
Harrison, NJ 07029
(201) 481-0600
(Asphalt roofing; metal siding)

The Barn People
Box 4
South Woodstock, VT 05071
(802) 457-3356
(Wood-based siding)

Bender Roof Tile Industries, Inc.
Box 190
Belleview, FL 34421
(800) 888-7074
(904) 245-7074
(Cement roof tile)

Berridge Manufacturing Co.
1720 Maury Street
Houston, TX 77026
(800) 231-8127
(Metal roofing)

Bird, Inc.
Bird Roofing Division
1077 Pleasant Street
Norwood, MA 02062
(800) BIRD-INC (NE only)
(617) 551-0656
(Asphalt shingles)

C&H Roofing, Inc.
Country Cottage Roof
Box 2105
Lake City, FL 32056
(800) 327-8115
(Wood roofing)

Cal-Shake, Inc.
Box 2265
5355 N. Vincent Avenue
Irwindale, CA 91706
(800) 736-7663
(818) 969-3451
(Masonry roofing)

Carter Holt Harvey Roofing USA, Inc.
773 Bradfield
Houston, TX 77060
(713) 931-4032
(Metal roofing)

Cedar Valley Shingle Systems
943 San Felipe Road
Hollister, CA 95023
(800) 521-9523
(408) 636-8110
(Wood-shingle panel siding)

Celotex Corp.
Box 31602
Tampa, FL 33631
(813) 873-1700
(Asphalt shingles)

CertainTeed Corp.
Box 860
750 E. Swedesford Road
Valley Forge, PA 19482
(800) 274-8530
(215) 341-7000
(Asphalt shingles)

Cladwood Division
Smurfit Newsprint
427 Main Street
Oregon City, OR 97045
(800) 547-6633
(Wood-based siding)

Classic Products, Inc.
Box 701
Piqua, OH 45356
(800) 543-8938
(Metal roofing and siding)

Dryvit Systems
One Energy Way
West Warwick, RI 02893
(800) 556-7752
(401) 822-4100
(Stucco-like siding systems)

DuPont Co., Tyvek
Chestnut Run Plaza
Laurel Run
Wilmington, DE 19880
(800) 448-9835
(Housewrap)

Elk Corp.
14643 Dallas Parkway
Suite 1000
Dallas, TX 75240
(214) 851-0400
(Asphalt roofing)

Eternit, Inc.
Box 679
Excelsior Industrial Park
Blandon, PA 19510
(800) 233-3155
(215) 926-0100
(Masonry roofing)

Evergreen Slate Co., Inc.
Box 248
68 E. Potter Avenue
Granville, NY 12832
(518) 642-2530
(Masonry roofing)

Fabrel Group Headquarters
3449 Hempland Road
Lancaster, PA 17601
(717) 397-2741
(Metal roofing and siding)

FibreCem Corp.
Box 411368
Charlotte, NC 28241
(800) 346-6147
(Masonry roofing)

Flying B Stone Co.
206 Blodgett Camp Road
Hamilton, MT 59840
(406) 363-3418
(Molded aggregate siding)

Follansbee Steel
Terne Division
Box 610
Follansbee, WV 26037
(800) 624-6906
(304) 527-1260
(Terne-coated metal roofing)

GAF Building Materials Corp.
1361 Alps Road
Wayne, NJ 07470
(201) 628-3000
(Asphalt roofing)

Georgia Pacific
Box 105605
133 Peachtree Street N.E.
Atlanta, GA 30348
(800) 447-2882
(Asphalt roofing; vinyl siding)

Gerard Roofing Technologies
955 Columbia Street
Brea, CA 92621
(800) 841-3213
(714) 529-0407
(Metal roofing)

Green River
Box 515
Sumas, WA 98295
(800) 663-8707
(Wood roofing and siding)

Historic Oak Roofing
Summit Towers, Suite 913
201 Locust Street
Knoxville, TN 37902
(800) 321-3781
(Wood roofing)

Impression
22599 S. Western Avenue
Torrance, CA 90501
(310) 618-1299
(Masonry roofing)

James Hardie
Building Products, Inc.
10901 Elm Avenue
Fontana, CA 92337
(800) 426-4051
(800) 942-7343
(Fiber cement roofing)

Lifetile Corp.
3511 N. Riverside Avenue
Rialto, CA 92376
(714) 822-4407
(Masonry roofing)

Louisiana-Pacific Corp.
111 S.W. Fifth Avenue
Portland, OR 97204
(800) 547-6331
(503) 221-0800
(Wood-based roofing and siding)

Ludowici-Celadon, Inc.
Box 69
New Lexington, OH 43764
(800) 945-8453
(614) 342-1995
(Masonry roofing)

Manville/Schuller
Box 5108
Denver, CO 80217
(800) 654-3103
(Asphalt roofing)

Marley Roof Tiles
1990 E. Riverview Drive
San Bernardino, CA 92408
(800) 344-2875
(714) 796-8324
(Masonry roofing)

Masonite Corp.
1 S. Wacker Drive, 36th Floor
Chicago, IL 60606
(312) 750-0900
(Asphalt roofing; hardboard
siding)

MaxiTile, Inc.
17141 S. Kingsview Avenue
Carson, CA 90746
(800) 338-8453
(310) 217-0316
(Masonry roofing)

Met-Tile,Inc.
Box 4268
Ontario, CA 91761
(800) 899-0311
(909) 947-0311
(Metal roofing)

Monier, Inc.
1745 Sampson Avenue
Corona, CA 91719
(800) 344-2875
(714) 750-5366
(Masonry roofing)

**Owens-Corning Fiberglas
Corp.**
Fiberglas Tower
Toledo, OH 43659
(419) 248-7074
(Asphalt roofing; vinyl siding)

**Panel Brick
Manufacturing, Inc.**
Box 907
1120 Ewing Road
Owensboro, KY 42302
(502) 684-7268
(Brick siding)

Plylap Industries
1462-D Tanforan Avenue
Woodland, CA 95776
(916) 661-0812
(Wood-based siding)

Real Brick Products, Inc.
3584 Bath Road
Perry, MI 48872
(800) 447-7440
(517) 625-6000
(Brick siding)

Reinke Shakes
3321 Willowwood Circle
Lincoln, NE 68506
(800) 228-4312
(Metal roofing and siding)

Revere Copper Products, Inc.
Box 300
Rome, NY 13442
(800) 448-1776
(315) 338-2022
(Metal roofing)

Rocky Mountain Log Homes
1883 Highway 93 South
Hamilton, MT 59840
(406) 363-5680
(Log siding)

Shakertown
Box 400
Winlock, WA 98596
(800) 426-8970
(206) 785-3501
(Wood roofing and siding)

**Simpson Timber Co.
Olympic Panel Products**
Third & Franklin Streets
Shelton, WA 98584
(800) 445-2442
(206) 427-8154
(Wood-based siding)

STO Industries
6175 Riverside Drive S.W.
Atlanta, GA 30331
(800) 221-2397
(404) 346-3666
(Stucco-like siding systems)

**Supradur Manufacturing
Corp.**
Box 908
Rye, NY 10580
(800) 223-1948
(914) 967-8230
(Masonry roofing)

Tegola USA
3807 Inwood Landing
Orlando, FL 32812
(800) 545-4140
(Metal and asphalt roofing)

US Gypsum Corp./Durock
Box 6721
Chicago, IL 60680
(800) 347-1345
(Stucco-like siding systems;
gypsum sheathing)

**Vincent Metals
Building Products Division**
724 24th Avenue S.E.
Minneapolis, MN 55414
(800) 328-7772
(612) 378-1131
(Metal roofing)

WESTILE
8311 W. Carder Court
Littleton, CO 80125
(800) 433-8453
(303) 791-1711
(Masonry roofing)

**Weyerhaeuser Co.
Hardboard Siding Division**
Box 9
Klamath Falls, OR 97601
(503) 883-4853
(Wood-based siding)

Wolverine Technologies
Box 537901
Livonia, MI 48153
(800) 521-9020
(313) 953-1100
(Vinyl siding)

W.P. Hickman Co.
Box 15005
Asheville, NC 28813
(704) 274-4000
(Metal roofing)

Zappone Manufacturing
N. 2928 Pittsburg
Spokane, WA 99207
(509) 483-6408
(Metal roofing)

ASSOCIATIONS

**American Hardboard
Association**
1210 W. Northwest Highway
Palatine, IL 60067
(708) 934-8800

**American Plywood
Association**
Box 11700
7011 S. 19th Street
Tacoma, WA 98411
(206) 565-6600

American Wood Council
1111 19th Street N.W.
Washington, DC 20036
(202) 463-2700

**Asphalt Roofing
Manufacturers Association**
6000 Executive Boulevard
Suite 201
Rockville, MD 20852
(301) 231-9050

Brick Institute of America
11490 Commerce Park Drive
Reston, VA 22091
(703) 620-0010

Building Stone Institute
Box 507
Purdys, NY 10578
(914) 232-5725

**California Redwood
Association**
405 Enfrente Drive, Suite 200
Novato, CA 94949
(415) 382-0662

**Cedar Shake & Shingle
Bureau**
515 116th Avenue N.E.
Suite 275
Bellevue, WA 98004
(206) 453-1323

Single-Ply Roofing Institute
20 Walnut Street, Suite 8
Wellesley Hills, MA 02181
(617) 237-7879

**Society of the Plastics
Industry
Vinyl Siding Institute
Division**
355 Lexington Avenue
New York, NY 10017
(212) 351-5400

**Southern Forest Products
Association**
Box 641700
Kenner, LA 70064
(504) 443-4464

**Western Red Cedar Lumber
Association**
1200–555 Burrard Street
Vancouver, BC V7X 1S7
Canada
(604) 684-0266

**Western Wood Products
Association**
Yeon Bldg.
522 S.W. Fifth Avenue
Portland, OR 97204
(503) 224-3930

INDEX